WALK IN YOUR POWER

WALK IN YOUR POWER

Kanina Johnson

PUBLISHING

For information on distribution rights, royalties, derivative works or licensing opportunities on behalf of this content or work, please contact the publisher at the address below or via email info@nolimitpublishinggroup.com.

COMPANIES, ORGANIZATIONS, INSTITUTIONS, AND INDUSTRY PUBLICATIONS: Quantity discounts are available on bulk purchases of this book for reselling, educational purposes, subscription incentives, gifts, sponsorship, or fundraising. Special books or book excerpts can also be created to fit specific needs such as private labeling with your logo on the cover and a message from a VIP printed inside.

No Limit Publishing Group
123 E Baseline Road, D-108
Tempe AZ 85283
info@nolimitpublishinggroup.com

This book was printed in the United States of America

No Limit Publishing
No Limit Enterprises, LLC
1601 E 69th Street, Suite 200
Sioux Falls, SD 57108

DEDICATION

I dedicate *Walk in Your Power* to my mom, whom I last spoke to on my 38th birthday. She passed away the next day. I now realize you did all you understood to love and care for me.

I dedicate *Walk in Your Power* to all those who desire to understand the truth of life.

CONTENTS

PREFACE

Thanks for taking the time to read my book! It's crazy as I do not have a clue how you found this book, but I believe there are no coincidences in life. The good news is no matter how you found *Walk in Your Power*, I am going to share with you some very valuable information that could literally change your life for the better!

I *am* living on purpose and feel blessed to be awakened to my God given power to enlighten people who desire a higher level of awareness of life: empowerment!

It is my life's purpose to empower people to love and accept themselves by being who they really are. It is my passion to teach others who desire change in their life emotionally, physically, spiritually, and financially: to teach them to create their dreams and live a life they love!

I love to help empower people to become awakened to life—to live in the now!

I love to help you learn how to rely on and believe in your unlimited potential and power, consciously learning how to ask, believe, and receive whatever your heart desires.

I am delighted to be in a position to assist you in achieving whatever it is that you want. I will let you in on the secret that the top 5% of the wealthy know. I searched! Guess what? I found the answers!

So far, I have spent more than 17 years studying the mind. I realized that the gap between potential and achievement could be bridged, if only people understood the power and potential of their own minds and made a decision to be, do, or have whatever they wished.

I spent 11 of those years working directly with mentally challenged people as a licensed Living Skills instructor and a licensed administrator, operating my own group home. For six of those years I worked for someone else's company as a direct staff member, then moved my way into management. I thought: I'm the one doing the work and receiving the knowledge; I should start my own business. Which I did!

I have owned and operated four successful businesses since 1996: a carpet cleaning company, a property management/real estate investment firm, a group home, and I have been a personal development/life success coach.

I have a loving and joyful marriage; my husband "soul mate" and I have been together since 1987—24 years and counting! I know I'm blessed to have met and recognized my soul mate just three and a half months after my 18th birthday.

I am a proud mother of three magnificent children; I gave birth to my first child in 1989, my second child in 1990, and my third child in 2001.

I had a strong intense desire that was compelling me. In 2004, I started diligently to search for life answers. I wanted to know the science of life. I wanted to know the truth of life. I found the answers after years of research through seminars, books, private courses, personal mentors, personal coaches, and thousands of dollars spent. I loved every second! I was so amazed with what I discovered I was compelled to become a certified life success coach and author to share what I learned with the world.

So, what really made me seek?

As a very young child, I was sexually abused by my stepdad from age 6 until I was 14 years old, at which point I understood how to fight back and protect myself. I lived a fearful life as a timid child. Some may ask, how did God let this happen? Well, I searched for the answer. Yes, I found it. My stepdad was undeveloped in his God given power, reacting to life in sleep mode. I was undeveloped in my God given power as a child. God had given the power to me, and I was not aware of the power. Yes, I have forgiven him!

I graduated from high school in 1986 and have been on my own since I was 17½ years old. I worked and attended a business trade school for a short period of time.

When I met my "soul mate" a year later, we both worked very hard to achieve the best in life. Which we did! Friends loved to be in our company. Unfortunately our apartment became the party spot. We began to party constantly, losing sight of our vision. Things fell apart, and our life became a nightmare. But my soul mate and I stayed together, no matter what. One day we decided to move 3,000 miles away from that surrounding to begin over.

We moved to California with $37. Yeah, you read it right: 37 DOLLARS! And a 5 month old baby. We arrived on Valentine's Day. We both immediately found work to earn money to support ourselves. The city bus was our method of transportation. While waiting at the bus stops, every vehicle looked good, I thought! After five months of riding the bus, we brought a car.

Later that year I gave birth to our second child. I remember being pregnant, craving a pizza but not having $5 to spare for Thursday night pizza special. I remember being pregnant and craving spaghetti and having to wait to get my food stamps. But through it all, I continually gave thanks and praise to God. I never lost sight of love and gratitude.

The first two years in California were a struggle. My soul mate and I continued to work very hard. We were determined to strengthen our family. I continually gave thanks!

In the third year, I received housing assistance; I worked full time and went to nursing assistance school.

One day, I decided that I did not want to live in poverty. I would not raise my children in poverty. I started to apply myself efficiently. My soul mate asked me to marry him after six years of togetherness. I gave my housing assistance up after only 12 months. I wrote my caseworker a letter thanking that person for the help and stating that I wished my slot to go to someone who really needed the help.

At the time of our private wedding ceremony, I told my grandmom I wanted to live in the area where our ceremony was held, which was considered the nicer side of town. And I wanted a four bedroom house with a pool.

Once we were married, we moved into a three bedroom rental house with a pool. My husband and I became foster parents, in addition to raising our own two kids. My husband worked days and I worked nights.

After living in that house for a year and a half, we were asked to move out of the house because a freeway was being built, and the state needed the lot where our house was located. We were given $11,000 to move.

We tried to purchase our own home, but the loan was denied. We moved into another rental house. This time, in the area of town where I desired to live. We continued to work hard, and we still were foster parents. We still tried to purchase our own house for a year and a half but continued to have the loan denied.

We didn't give up. Guess what? We finally were approved, and we still had our $11,000 that we used to go toward the down payment. I purchased my dream home, four bedrooms, with an in ground swimming pool in the area of town I desired. We purchased our first home when I was 27. A few months afterward, we started our first business, a carpet cleaning business.

Yes, we still were foster parents, we still worked hard. Three years later I started my group home business. I opened my home and heart to the mentally challenged.

Several years later, I began to invest in real estate, providing nice homes in nice areas to low income females who were receiving housing assistance. I also provided inspiration naturally to each of them.

What I came to realize is how much I've loved helping others. I naturally desire to help others become their best. I realized people would gravitate toward me. I realized I was speaking words of empowerment to whomever I speak with. I realized my God given purpose was to empower others.

I have dedicated my life to helping others!

I'm writing this book 20 years after arriving in California and 14 years after purchasing my first home at the age of 27. I'm sitting in my home office writing this book. In that house!

Here's the moral of the story. I was physically struggling, but I kept my mind on what I desired and loved. I helped others and continually gave thanks to God. I was not operating from fear. I was operating from love. Guess what? To tell you the truth I really did not know what I was doing. As I looked back, I went from struggle to success unconsciously.

However, I can tell you for sure: Doing my in depth research of life, I realized I was doing everything that was being revealed to me. It was like, "oh my God, that is what I have been doing." The secret of life. Guess what? I'm revealing that knowledge in *Walk in Your Power*. What I wrote about is happening in our life if we know it or not. I want you to know so you can live your life with purpose and passion.

Love empowerment!

INTRODUCTION: MEET KANINA

Kanina, what inspired you to write *Walk in Your Power*?

For many years I searched for spiritual answers desiring to understand who is God, the reason I am on earth, why are we humans here, and other questions like that. And I know many others have those questions, wanting to gain the knowledge and understanding. I discovered the answers. And I love to share them.

Walk in Your Power will give you the answers and practical ways to live the life you love.

For now, I will give you a brief insight. God is "Spirit" Love, and we "spirits" are here on earth to love and help one another, co create with God. We must recognize the power within us is God and consciously identify ourselves with God. We all have been given a specific purpose for our life and only you can discover your purpose. This Earth operates by natural laws, and these natural universe laws are operating in your life whether you know it or not.

As I refer to the term God I'm not speaking from a religious stand point. I'm speaking about truly understanding your oneness with God the intelligence mind that knows all…

You may see God as, Love, Universe, Divine Mind, Lord, Jehovah, Divine Intelligence, and other names; it's your choice. I prefer to say God. All those terms mean one and the same thing. I have learned to call God working in my life, *Law*.

As we strive to work with the Law of life we are living closer to God, which brings us a better understanding. He is as close to us as the breath we breathe.

We must strive to be on the outside what we visualize on the inside. Your thoughts make you who you are; your ideals, principles or your ruling desire will determine your destiny.

I want everyone that desires to understand why he or she is here on earth to get a clear understanding that he or she has been given power and how to use that power. You must learn to use your power unless you wish to be used by it. You must make an effort everyday to use the knowledge you have gained.

I want all to understand how to use their thinking faculties, to master their mind and guide it with intelligence, to learning to think as they ought to. Which is truth!

You can gain this ability by studying the law of life. Then give constant effort to your thinking faculties as you work with these laws. Have good and sound reasons for all the views you hold.

I will help you learn to train your mind to clear and exact thinking. Then your ability to do so on your own will grow faster by regular exercise and discipline, so that, you may live your life daily thinking more constructive and good thoughts, about yourself, others, and all natural things.

There is only good. We all are good people; however, some of us do not have such good habits and behaviors. A lot of us are still asleep. I choose to understand that when someone displays negative talk and actions, that person is behaving unconsciously. If that individual were awake, consciously aware, I think he or she would truly handle the situation with love.

I choose to be the product, of the product, meaning I live my life by the law of life.

I have learned from great masters such as Bob Proctor, Mary Morrissey, Earl Nightingale, Raymond Holliwell, Napoleon Hill, Wallace D. Wattles, and others.

What do you think is the most important thing someone must understand to help raise his or her level of awareness faster?

A person must understand how the mind functions. The mind is movement in our body. We have two parts to the mind: conscious and subconscious.

The conscious mind is our thinking mind, our educated mind. It is the part that thinks and reasons. Our free will resides here. We have five senses, the ability to see, hear, smell, taste, and touch. These senses are connected to our conscious mind. We can choose our thoughts and originate ideas. We have the ability to accept or reject any thoughts that come to our mind. No person or circumstance can cause you to think about thoughts or ideas you do not choose. All pain, pleasure, abundance, or limitation is either originated in your conscious mind or accepted unconsciously from an outside source.

As you accept a thought, it is impressed upon the second part of your personality, your subconscious mind. Even though your conscious mind chose to accept the thought, this part must also accept it. This part of the mind has no ability to reject. We must be careful how we speak to ourselves. Any thought that is repeatedly impressed upon our subconscious mind will become a habit. It has no ability to know the different between what is real or imagined. This is your power center, the God like part of you referred to as spirit. It functions in every cell of your body. This part of you operates in an orderly manner, by law. This orderly manner is through feelings and actions. It affects the most visible and obvious part of you, although it is actually the smallest part you: your body. This is the physical you, the house your "spirit" lives in. It is the instrument of the mind. The thoughts or images you consciously choose will automatically be impressed upon your subconscious and then move your body into action. The actions you are involved with, determine your results.

You have a thought, which gives you a feeling, which move your body into action, then you get a result.

All things and events, all experiences and conditions of life, are results.

Kanina you have been speaking about the law working in our lives. How can we be sure the law will work for everyone?

We're here to create. I'm talking creating a better world. First for ourselves, and then for everyone we come into contact with. Everything we desire and face must submit to the law of life.

Your life will improve as you deepen your understanding, explore the concepts, and begin to live in harmony with the laws that govern the universe.

A lot of people are aware of the film *The Secret*, which has created awareness worldwide of the law of attraction. I have come to understand that the law of attraction has always been here. I will speak about the law of attraction more in detail later. But I want to give you something to think about. The secret to life is: we become what we think about!

It doesn't take any more effort to go after what you may call a big idea than it does to go after a small one. When you are working with the law, nothing is big and nothing is small. I will be helping you to understand how to work with the law. And when you do, your whole life begins to move in harmony with God's laws.

I see the law as the uniform and orderly method of God. It is how things are done. We are created in God's image and here on earth to do God's work. God's work is creation. Since God is the creator and we are co-creators, we were given creative faculties: reason, intuition, perception, will, memory, and imagination. I will be explaining each later.

As you grow in knowledge and are able to form better ideas and better opinions, do not hesitate to change your views. I would like you to test the things you hear me say. Don't accept or disregard the ideas without testing them. At least, give yourself the opportunity to apply the ideas. Remember this quote: "The wise man changes his mind, the fool never." You will never have progress without change. For all of us there must be a constant stream of new thoughts, better thoughts and truer thoughts to ensure progression in our lives. Once you perceive the better, let go of the old.

Once you feel something, think something, and know something is more life giving, discard the old idea and opinion and proceed. You should proceed to using your creative thinking faculties, which I will explain later, because one of two things will happen. Either you will master your mind and guide it intelligently, or your mind will master you and then only produce the programs that have been installed in it, which are coming from a world that operates from lack and limited thinking.

As you work with the ideal of that which you would seek to bring forth and the practical, which is the application of the laws, and as you study and apply the laws I will be speaking about, you can absolutely count on your life producing the results you have planted. You will become aware that all our problems are mental in nature. They have no existence outside of themselves.

As you hold a good and sound reason for your viewpoints, many of your old views will fall to pieces. Form clear and definite ideas regarding your firm beliefs: why you do as you do, and why you think as you think. This practice is like conducting a mental housecleaning.

The practice of clear thinking clarifies the mind, tones up the faculties, sharpens your perceptions, and will give you a stronger and better grasp of the basic essentials for a larger and richer life.

What is a sure means to advance on the material as well as the spiritual planes of life?

Clear and exact thinking is a great necessity. It's truly a sure means to advance in the material world and the spiritual world. You must make a distinction between mere surface thought, which is ordinary and commonplace thinking, and real thought, which is associated with the understanding of truth. Real thought is deep thinking, which stirs inactive powers to action, quickens your perception, and leads to increased understanding. The ordinary thinking is passing of mental activity.

The little depth surface thought that we give to the ordinary and small things of daily life is not the thought that is going to transform your life or your character, develop your mind, or change your destiny. It is not the real thought.

Your inner convictions control your desires and motives. They determine the course of your life and your personal destiny. We all are controlled by our convictions, our fixed beliefs.

The positive deep penetrating thought comes from a strong conviction born out of a higher perception and a clearer realization of the truth, which comes from your heart. It will lead to a steady increase of your power and your authority and will make your life more meaningful and fulfilling. It requires some highly constructive effort. Something will become clearer to you than ever before.

Kanina, one of the most important questions today is whether we have the capacity and power to control our life. Millions of people are now being affected by unemployment, losing their homes to foreclosure, and poverty. There are a lot of problems. How can you help us solve those problems?

First of all, everything goes back to understanding how your mind functions and understanding your God given power.

ʃ

Some of us are not sure that we create our circumstances. When you listen to the news and confront all the negative outside influence, then you focus on that negativity, hoping it doesn't happen to you. Guess what? You are impressing those negative circumstances upon your subconscious mind, and the universe will give you more negativity to deal with, meaning you are letting others create your circumstances.

When we submit to that kind of believing, the circumstances around us become stronger than the power that is within us. Then we become defeated before the race begins.

But you must realize that there is a wonderful world of power, possibility, and promise within us. Within us is the mind, and the mind is the creative source of all that transpires in the experience and the life of you and me.

You are the master of your circumstance. Speak your power! Lead! Create! Fate is in your hands! Determine it.

You have the power to create your life by design. That's right! You have power! First you must take responsible for all that happens in your life.

Here are four things you must do to accept personal responsibility. Once you accept the responsibility for these things in your life, you are on your way to your dream life.

- Every thought you think
- Every feeling/emotion you feel
- Every action you take
- Every result in your life

If you do not accept those four things in your life, you have no choose but to be a victim. You will stay stuck in the same place.

I understand that you are saying all the conditions in our lives are the results of our actions. All our actions are the outcome of our ideas. Then that means our ideas must determine the condition of our lives.

Yes, an idea is a thought or a group of thoughts. An idea is an image or a picture in the mind. All conditions are the result of our actions, and all actions are the outcome of our ideas. Our ideas determine the conditions in our daily lives.

I like to refer to this power as spirit or energy. If we are not consciously and purposely giving it direction, then other people and circumstances—the outside world—are going to give it direction. That is where confusion takes over and produces confused results.

I remember becoming aware of this powerful truth. It was like "wow!" I realized I was living in an unconscious state of mind, and I desired to be awakened. I started to realize life is proceeding through me and by me. The way I shape my ideas changes my experience.

When you experience something you do not like, pause, take a deep breath, and then consciously choose what you would make out of the experience, rather than what that experience will make out of you.

Every person is his or her own designer. Every idea and mental picture must produce after its own kind, no matter if the picture is good or bad. The law determines it. The law does not question or challenge what kind of picture you give it.

A mental photograph is just like a photograph that is taken of you, someone else, or an object; it produces exactly what it sees. Therefore, negative destroying ideas cannot produce constructive and positive results.

As we begin to absorb these mental pictures in our mind, we consciously or unconsciously exercise a power to produce them. The creative process will continue to work day and night. It does not stop until the idea is completed. We cannot picture thoughts of poverty, failures, or disease and expect in return to enjoy wealth, success, or great health.

Many people are planning to gain heaven at some future time, after they are decreased, no longer physically living on this planet, when it is actually a condition and a state of mind that can be had now as hereafter. In fact, unless it is gained here on earth and now, it can never be had in the future.

You say all people are governed by law, whether they know it or not. I think this is possibly the same idea that some people have concerning prayer.

Many people blame God when they do not get the answer they were seeking. Yes, I think it's possibly the same idea that some have concerning prayer. They think it is God's fault, will, or desire that they did not get the answer they were seeking. They use God as their excuse when they are unable to explain some act of nature.

You must realize it is only your fault if your prayers are unanswered. The creative law is always ready to answer and cannot fail to respond when approached rightly and wisely. The moment a person is able to contact and realize the law, that individual will at once enjoy the benefits.

The nonphysical level of life is always moving into physical form. The physical level of life is the manifestation of the nonphysical. Prayer is the movement that takes place between spirit and form with and through you.

I have come to realize, when I pray for one thing and then fear and doubt that I will receive it, that I then scatter my mental forces and can only attract what my lesser thoughts believe and expect.

You know it is the realization of the law in action that will determine what you manifest. We must understand everything happens by law, whether we like it or not. The entire universe operates in a very exact way.

We have a limited level of conscious awareness. But we are involved deeply in a mind that knows all, and that mind contains all knowledge and all truth; it is seeking to give us this knowledge. This limitless wisdom and power is open to everyone. You can draw from it as you will and according to your needs.

You can make yourself what you desire to "be"; you can do what you wish to "do"; you can "have" what you want. If you really desire to be, do, and have all that your heart desires, you must become aware of your oneness with God, so you may perceive truth, have wisdom, and know the right ends to seek and the right means to use to attain those ends. And, of course, so that you may secure power and ability to use the means.

There is a science to thinking about everything, which will prevent needless waste of mental energy and produce the desired results.

It is necessary for each of us to learn to give intelligent direction to the creative powers of our mind, so that we may obtain the best and the most life giving results in a specific area of expression, like our business, relationships, health, and finances. In whatever area we want to activate and amplify so that we may experience more freedom and fulfillment, we must learn. It is really up to you and it is up to me to learn the proper way to give intelligent direction to the creative power that is moving through and within me and you now.

The small mind does not need to remain small or undeveloped. It can grow and expand and then eventually become great. The path is clear and simple. Just form your own clear conceptions and firm beliefs from the highest point of view you can reach, then think and act accordingly. It is a natural sequence for advancement to follow. The mind is no greater than its conceptions.

As we learn to improve and enlarge our ideas, our mental pictures, so that we can improve and enlarge our thinking, our life falls into form. I will be helping you understand how to do this later. This is what *Walk in Your Power* is all about: helping you gain an understanding that there is a law of life and how to apply the laws that govern the universe in your life, for your greater good. As you become more aware, you will notice there is an orderly sequence to the progression of life. The universe is spiral. Our

f

DNA is spiral; there is the pull of becoming that is occurring throughout the universe. That pull of becoming is in all of us calling our awareness upward in the spiral of becoming. And the way we will move upward is being true to that pull of becoming.

It speaks to each of us in a unique way, to our own level of consciousness and where we are at the time of hearing that pull. It might speak to you about longing for a relationship to be better or free from struggle. It might speak to you about your health and freedom from pain, about wanting freedom from financial limitations. That pull of becoming upward will speak to you in a language you will understand. It is agreeing with the life you are living and the possibility of a greater expanded version of life expressing itself through you.

Okay, Kanina! The will of the law is forever a greater expression and freedom. The law of life is at work in you and me. What happens when our intention becomes in harmony and cooperation with the universal intention?

When our intention becomes in harmony and cooperation with the universal intention, we have become an expression of that good because there is a way to work with the law of life and not fight the current of becoming. Do not force but work with the current of becoming. When your intention is the same as the universal intention and you are not just trying to do something for yourself, but you understand that we all are a part of something that is extraordinary, that's always existing and unlimited, meaning we all are connected to something that is magnificent, eternal, infinite, and good. When you achieve that understanding, your life can be an expression of that good.

We must really understand that all our failures in life are due to limits and lack around us, that we are letting others and outside circumstances affect our life. It's living from the outside, which is the worldly way, and it is controlling us.

Success and happiness come to us when we are taking sides with the infinite intelligence, the law, the spirit, the God within us. When you are living your life in this manner on purpose, you are taking the law into your mind, which lives as a silent partner. You then have become consciously aware of the source, the creator of all power, and you receive the benefits that surround all of us.

I know this to be real, to have the law of life, the presence of all be a silent partner in all of us.

We must realize if we are searching or being greedy and looking for a shortcut to solving everything and we are not willing to learn, grow, think differently, and work with the law of life, then this power I'm speaking about will not work for you.

Living with all the strong evidences is something that does not just happen to a few people. We all have life energy. You must seek your awareness and the direction for the good that is in and around you. So that it will be made to manifest through you in an exceptional way that is unique to what it is that occurs and feels good to you, to be good.

We each have the capacity to bring forth what we will; we hold the power. It can be great or small because we can think. In our thinking, we create desires and ideas.

We have power, the universal power of mind, which is endowed within every one of us and all creation. All that we desire can be ours if we ask, understand the law of life, and apply it correctly.

We must remember God, the master over all, the power of this universe, sent us into a far and distant land, which we refer to as earth and human birth, to accomplish one specific task: to discover who we really are.

We are actually sons and daughters of this universe, we are heirs, we have been given dominion of this universe, we are life itself, in all its glory, beauty, and power. But if you choose not to discover and be who you really are, at the end, it will be as if you had done nothing.

There is a universal law to the way we think. Give us a clear understanding how to get this law to work in our lives.

The universal law of thinking. I love this law, and I think it is one of the most important laws that we are going to understand and apply. In the Bible, it states in Proverbs, "As a man thinketh in his heart, so is he." That tells us our attention should be given to our predominant mental state. Thus, the thoughts you think about the most are what have power and authority over your life. This is the foundation of your life. Stop and take a moment to think about that because it is truly the first step to freedom. Be aware of what you are thinking. Thoughts are the beginning of the creative process. When you get a clear understanding and then apply the knowledge into your own life, you will have upward positive thinking, which is the quickest and easiest way to unleash a positive rush that will quickly attract to you events, circumstances, and people to help you accomplish your desires. This is what some people may refer to as coincidences.

Many of us allow negative thoughts to stop our flow of good thoughts. I refer to this situation as a blessing blocker. By increasing your awareness of this powerful universal law, you will master the secret to do away with negative thoughts forever.

We are naturally programmed by our genetics and our environment; we have become the product of somebody else's fixed way of thinking; we have become their habits. When we were young kids, our subconscious mind was undeveloped. The ideas, thoughts, and images of our parents, teachers, and other authority leaders were impressed upon the subconscious part of our mind. Someone else is controlling our thinking until we get to the point where we understand that we actually have control over our own life. No one else nor the economy can control you, unless you consciously or unconsciously choose not to take control.

To the average person, life is a deep mystery. If your life is a mystery to you, you are considered ignorant. All things are mysteries when they are not understood.

)

The mind is the basic factor and governing power in the human race. Until we get to the point where we start to understand our mind, we truly do not have control over our life. But it is actually simple.

As you clearly understand how to think properly, you will open the door to freedom. Begin to pay attention to what you are thinking. As your level of awareness rises, you will notice what you are thinking and what you predominantly focus on will begin to manifest and show itself in your everyday life. Your life will no longer be a mystery.

We are spiritual beings, living in a physical body, who have been gifted with an intellect. We have the ability to think and reason differently from any other life form on Earth. We are the highest life form created, that we are aware of. The way we choose to use our intellect, which is "our God given ability" to think and reason, will govern our emotional state.

This also applies to our imagination and creative thinking.

As children we are extremely creative. As we get older, we cover our creative potential mainly because of concern about what others think of us or think that imagining is stupid and not real.

You now are aware of the importance of using your imagination. Awaken your imagination to dream and develop ideas.

When we learn to use our mind for advancement, we are using correctly these hidden powers, forces, and faculties. This is the key to success in living life.

This is part of our open door to freedom: understanding the experience of the power of thinking. As we think, so our life becomes.

Now everyone thinks. What is so special about having to think in a certain way?

You know everyone does think! They think they are thinking, and the truth is many people really do not. They are having a lot of mental activities going on, which is not thinking. Thinking is done in our conscious mind, our intellectual mind, which connects to our five senses. We see, hear, smell, taste, and touch. A very large amount of information enters our conscious mind, so our mind is constantly busy all the time. A lot of people believe this is thinking; this is not thinking; this is your mind being busy.

Your greatness is attained only by constantly thinking great thoughts. You cannot become great in your outward personality until you are great internally. You cannot become great internally until you begin to think properly. No amount of formal education, study, or reading can make you great without thought. But your thoughts can make you great with very little study. You are mentally developed by what you think about what you read, not by what you read.

Greatness is inherent in everyone and may be manifested by all. Everyone may become great. If you desire to become great, the soul must act and must rule the mind and body. Our knowledge is limited; we fall into error through ignorance. If you desire to avoid this error, you must connect your soul with Universal Spirit.

From my intense thoughts after reading Wallace D. Wattles' books, I have come to believe Universal Spirit is the intelligent substance from which all things come; it is in and through all things. Hold on now! This is powerful! All things are known to this universal mind, and you can unite yourself with it. You will then enter into all knowledge. That is why you should make a decision to have, be, and do whatever your heart desires because you do not have to know how you will do it; you just have to know you will do, be, or have it. After you listen to your intuition and act, you may say, "How I did that?" Well guess what? That is the universal mind, your silent partner, giving you the answers.

All you know, all the power is within each of us! It is our own responsibility to tap into this power.

To understand how to stay connected to this power you must cast out everything that separates you from God. Like jealousy, envy, strife, gossip, and being hateful. You must will to live divine life and rise above all moral temptations. You must forsake all course of action that is not aligned with your highest ideals.

You must form a mental conception of yourself at the highest, and hold the conception until it becomes a habit, your thought-form. You must outwardly realize and express your thought-form in your actions. You must do everything you do in a great way. That includes dealing with your family, friends, neighbors, and acquaintances; every act must be an expression of your ideals. You will then have made yourself known and be recognized as a personality of power. You will receive knowledge by inspiration and will know all that you need to know. You will receive all material wealth you form in your thoughts. You will not lack for any good thing. Great works will seek you out, and all will be delighted to honor you. Wow! That is powerful!

We are a progressive being, a creature of constant growth, but you said only if we think. Why do we constantly get the same results?

If we are not properly thinking, we are not growing. That's why many people get the same results year after year. They are stuck. Now that's ignorance: doing the same thing and expecting different results.

The ruling mind is upward, positive, and aspiring. When your mind is constantly in that state, all forces will be directed into advance channels toward you. But if your state of mind is downward, in strife and negativity, all forces will be misdirected.

To begin to think upward, you must do what you really want to do. Strongly think about what you really want in life. I'm not talking about what you think you can get or what you think you can do. What do you really want?

To really get into what we want, we have to imagine, fantasize. Then turn the fantasy into a particular concept, into a theory, and that is when we really begin to think. If you desire to move upward, to grow, you will have to think. But you will have to direct your thoughts toward a result that you absolutely desire.

f

The truth is we can have anything we desire. Thrive to get a fully clear understanding of the laws governing the universe, our being. These laws will help move you toward what you want. That is exactly why I wrote *Walk in Your Power* to help you get that understanding with simplicity.

Focus on what you want with a clear image; the unseen forces will send you what you desire. Your mind is a powerful magnet and will attract whatever corresponds to its ruling state.

You speak about the difference between mental activity and genuine thinking. So you are saying that our understanding of genuine thinking is from our own creativity. What is it that is within us seeking expression?

It is the desire of universal intelligent "God." We "spiritual beings" are connected to "spirit" the infinite. Spirit is 100% evenly present in all places at the same time. There is no end; infinite is forever, so there is no death.

All men and women everywhere are good and perfect. All is right with the world. We are here on earth to unite with God for the completion of the perfect work. We all have a special gift. We all are unique, so there is something within us that wants to move to a higher level. And it is essential that we properly think. We are an instrument for spirit to flow through. We have a pure spirit flowing to and through us. Through our thinking, we take that flow and create thoughts. We take those thoughts and combine them with other thoughts, and then we form an idea. Pure ideas are thoughts directed towards a purpose. James Allen states, "Until thought is linked to purpose, there is no intelligent accomplishment."

Desire comes from the spiritual essence within us, desiring to express itself in a greater way.

If there is something we really desire and growth is not about getting things, then what is it about?

Growth is about the growth. We will get the things.

We have goals, and our goals are material in nature. You know we live in a physical body, and we communicate with a material world. Thus, it is natural that we have material goals. It is not the goal we are pursuing; it is the growth that we are going after. We should be spending our days doing what we love. We should be working for satisfaction because it is the means of putting to use our creative abilities.

I truly think a person should stop on a regular basic, and then take a look at his or her results. You should pay close attention to your behavior, realizing that your behavior pattern is nothing more than an expression of your thinking. If you desire to change your behavior pattern, because you do not like the results you are getting, then you must change your thinking.

We know if we change the way we are looking at something, the thing we are looking at will change because our point of view is the perspective that we gain from how we are thinking about the things and what we are looking at.

We must choose a direction that we are going in our life; only a small percentage of people do. A lot of people are just following other people, not realizing they are doing whatever is going on in their mind, which is nothing but confused thoughts. Whatever is going on outside is controlling what is going on inside.

I think that many people, including me, have had at times no idea that we're not thinking. We must realize we are just the patterns moving through our being that have been around us, that we inherited. And we have let those patterns run our life, not knowing that we had the capacity and power that we could had draw from that actually would be our true character.

ʄ

We are prone to believe more in what we see. Why do you think the evidence of the sense is the only facts some people will accept?

Seeing is believing appears to be more real to many people, but it is not truth. The truth is: believing is seeing. We must realize that what we believe determines what we see. What is invisible is more real than what the reflection of our eyes is projecting on the outside.

If someone chooses to live only by physical sight, that person's world is very small. Many defeats and failures are due to mental blindness. We truly see with the inner eye of understanding.

Our eyes deceive us. That is why it is very important to understand how to see with the inner eye, so that you will not be deceived.

The universe operates in a very orderly manner. We want to bring order to our understanding; as we bring order, we remove confusion. As confusion leaves, we are able to make new choices.

Therefore, I'm talking about an infinite power that operates in an orderly way. Because we think in pictures, we have the ability to choose the images. As we hold the image, we are getting emotionally involved, and that is what keeps us moving forward.

The power of our thoughts is present everywhere; this is difficult for many to believe. Although this power is invisible to the physical sight, it is an actual force like electricity. We all are surrounded by an ocean of thought stuff, which is circulating through the universe like electricity. We can flash our thoughts completely around the world, many times in less than a single second.

It does not take us any longer to think to Hawaii than it takes to think across the room. Thought waves are cosmic waves that are penetrating all time and space, and they are 100% evenly present in all places at the same time.

Understanding how to think properly, we are actually accessing infinite possibilities, drawing from them a particular idea out of a desire or being discontent.

Everything we desire is already here, so it is not the answers we should be looking for. It is the questions that we want to think about. It is the questions that are going to trigger the answers. Your answer comes with your question. You must understand that all this starts in our thinking. It is the way we think on an emotional level. It is what we are thinking about inside, not just in our intellect.

Kanina, elaborate more on what you mean by what we see, but our eyes are deceiving us.

It's just like standing on the beach and watching a ship sail slowly into the sea. It appears the ship is sinking, but our eyes are deceiving us.

We do not see with our eyes; our eyes are like a pair of windows. At the back of these windows are a reflector, and this reflector in turn forms an image of what you see. It then sets up a wave current that follows along thin wires that we refer to as nerves. Your nerves relay the image back to your brain. We refer to this part of the brain as the memory center. Therefore, if our picture is a common one, our memory accepts it quickly. If the picture is new, our memory does not recognize it. Then that picture has to be repeated several times until it makes a lasting impression. We actually see with our mind and see through our eyes.

We say terms like "black person" or "white person." There is neither a black or white person, compared to the actual color of black or white, like black shoes or a white shirt. The reason we say black or white person is because it has been programmed in our mind. Someone put it there. So we are seeing things that are not true.

Thus, when you are worried about challenges in your life, remind yourself that it may be an illusion of the senses.

ſ

So we have limitations programmed in; it is part of our being. You say we have to recognize that. And through our own intellect we've got to have the wisdom and understanding to change the programming in our own mind, or our life will not change!

You are right! We must begin to recognize what we are made of, which is very potent and powerful, and understand the power which has freely been given to us. Since many of us have very little understanding and experience of the power, our main thoughts are a life of struggles and difficulty. We must remember, as we think in our heart, we can create a life that could just as easily be one of joy and fulfillment because all along the power to change the thinking is within us.

We as individuals must understand if we are to get what we really want to get out of life—what we are promised—we must dedicate a certain part of each day to our own well-being. We must constantly invest time and money in ourselves. Our mind is our most valuable asset.

We speak about the difference between knowing about the law and knowing the law. Many people are brilliant and still live small lives.

The secret to get the law to work for you is to bring it from knowing about the law and the power of it to actually applying the promise, which you are doing when you look at your day and recognize that part of your day was devoted to yourself in a deeper realm of your own being.

You know thinking is not taught in the educational system. And thinking is a mighty force. Scientists compare thought with the speed of light. It is amazing; they tell us that light travels 186,000 miles per second. And our thoughts are traveling 930,000 times faster than the sound of our voice. At this point and time, no other force or power in the universe is as great or quicker. Thought is sudden. It is an unlimited force.

Pay close attention to when you do your best thinking. I do my best thinking early in the morning.

Our power to think determines our state of living. As you become more competent in your thinking, you will generate a power that travels far and near. This power sets up a radiation that becomes individual as you determine, as you attract on purpose. It is like a thought you constantly think about and then attract the same condition.

Since our thoughts affect our welfare and often can affect others that we think about, why does the kind of thoughts that we register in our memories or we habitually think attract the same kind of conditions?

If we take the thought of success and keep it in our mind, those thought components will be attracted; like attract like. We are mentally drawn to the universal thought flow of success. And that flow of success exists in all of us.

Then the psychic in us contacts the mind or minds of other people who are thinking along the same lines. Then later those minds are brought into our lives.

When we advance with confidence in the direction of our dream, it seem as though we pass an invisible boundary. All sort of things begin to occur in our life for the better.

Thus, when we are thinking along the line of success, we do not have to worry about the how. Because it will naturally come to us.

When you are aware of someone who is successful, just know successful minded people help success to come to them. It works both ways. A person who dwells on thoughts of poverty will gravitate toward poverty conditions. That person will draw people who also accept failure and poverty. It is sad, but they will accept it as a real part of their life. We must remember what the mind holds within takes it form in the outer world.

Some people think we must be dealing with two forces: To attract the good we must get rid of the bad, but that is not true. That is as if you were cold, you do not have to fight the cold. We would build up the warm by turning on the heater or building a fire. We do not work with the cold and heat the same to get warm.

Therefore, to get rid of the bad, we must focus on, resonate with, and become one with the ideas of that which we are seeking. We must raise our consciousness in what we are seeking to express. That is how you eliminate the bad.

Prosperity and poverty are not two different things. They are two sides of one and the same thing, just as one coin has two sides. We must turn our attention in the direction of our desires in order for the desire to be fulfilled. What we focus on will expand.

The law is evidenced in the way it works in nature. Nature does not distinguish between what seed it will receive; it grows whatever seed we plant. The universe is for our good.

You want to stop and pay attention to what is going on in your mind. You may not monitor your thinking, but you must pay attention to what is going on in your mind. When you take a look at your results, you will realize the mind is the cause of the problem.

We are constantly thinking. We can change our thoughts but cannot stop thinking. How do you understand this?

Thinking power flows in and through us like the air we breathe. We have the power to direct our power of thinking through constructive channels of expression. Scientists have stated that no power can act without producing some kind of an effect. By thinking, we continue to produce effects.

We continue to have something going on in our mind because our thoughts never stop flowing. You want to pay close attention where you are letting others anger you, where you are impatient or hold resentment because this is not orderly thinking. To have better conditions in our life, we must first make effort to organize our thoughts. The majority of people think at random, having no clarity in their mind in which to frame their thoughts. We must decide what we want and what results we want to get. For most of us, our thinking is out of control, chaotic, and unorganized; that is why we have disappointments and failures staying near us. We attract what we are thinking. If we want success, we must think it and become it. If we want to advance, we must make an effort to rise higher. To be truly happy, we must live our life in harmony and order.

If we were to follow some kind of steps because we desire to understand how to use the law when it comes to properly thinking, to shift our thinking to a higher order because we no longer want to practice just busy thinking, what could a person take from this lesson?

We must understand we have to bring order to our mind. We must have direction and then think thoughts that are moving in that direction. Many people do whatever comes along, and that will not work. Plan your day, and include something that will help you accomplish your goal.

If we are having problems, it is ourselves not controlling our own ideas. Having control over our own life consists of an organized thought direction. Plan your work and time so you are working steadily toward your goal. You should fill your day so full of productive duties that there is no room for waste of any kind to enter your mind.

The thing that has helped me the most is that I do not start my day until I speak with my supreme power, God. That communication is also known as prayer. I communicate with my supreme power through the day, as though I would communicate with a person. This is my silent partner. That is why you want to treat everyone with respect; you never know who has that silent partner as their best friend.

I list how I want my day to proceed. I want to be orderly in my thinking, nice and considerate of others, and stay focused. I manage my activities for the day by writing a to do list the night before and whenever I get a great thought. I manage my activities. I give myself a command when the time arrives actually to complete the task, which will bring great success. I write my constructive ideas on paper and then my thinking is focused toward directions that I have given myself.

Understanding how this great power of our thinking operates is wonderful, but actually to apply it in our own life is where the change happens. You have power; walk in it! Remember your thoughts become things!

1

ATTITUDE

" *Be the change you want to see in the world.*

–Mahatma Gandhi (1869–1948) "

DEFINITION OF ATTITUDE

Attitude is the composition of your thoughts, feelings, and actions. It is literally all three of these elements of your being added together. There is nothing about you that is not part of your attitude. Mentally, attitude provides a direction for success in our life. It is a choice. You can choose positive or negative. Good attitude, good results. Bad attitude, bad results.

It is our attitude toward life that will determine life's attitude toward us. We shape our own life, and the shape is determined by our attitude. If we have the attitude we cannot do something, we most likely will not do it. What we receive from life or fail to receive from life are due overall to our attitude.

We can alter our life by altering our attitude of mind. This is a measure of control that's given to us freely. The attitude we take toward ourself determines our attitude toward the world. Since we are so familiar with ourself, we take ourself for granted, not realizing things we can accomplish and goals we can reach, thinking others can accomplish things we cannot.

Attitude is the reflection, a result of a person's will. It is extremely powerful; it can bring us fabulous results. In order to attract those marvelous results, we must properly train it every day. It makes the difference between success and failure, great expectation, and the lack of it.

If you don't have a definition for what attitude is, you will have a difficult time changing it. Anything you lack clarity on, you will have a hard time changing, altering, or transforming. This is also true with your attitude. If you don't know what attitude is, how do you know if you have a good one or a bad one? And if you have a bad one, how do you change it?

Many people oppose changes in their life, living a defensive and dark life. People that live a joyful and youthful life welcome change; they see it for what it really is. Change is an open door to new opportunities and new chances for more fulfillment.

You have more control over that which you understand. The more you understand what attitude is and how to change it, the more control you will have over your attitude. If you lack an understanding of how to drive a car, you will have some big problems driving down the road. You will be totally out of control. The same goes with something as simple and seemingly unimportant as your attitude. An out of control attitude is just as dangerous as an out of control vehicle. Your attitude directs the most powerful piece of equipment on the planet—your mind. Let's build more of an understanding, so you can gain more control over your own power.

The more you control your attitude, the better life gets. The more you control your thoughts, feelings, and actions (attitude), the better you can predict your results. If your attitude is consistent and positive, you will consistently get positive results in your life. It is just that simple, and it works the same way in reverse.

ATTITUDE'S IMPACT

Your attitude is uniquely yours. Only you can change your attitude.

In every area of your life, attitude has an impact because your attitude is the cause of your results. One of the great universal laws is the law of cause and effect. Results are effects, and the cause is your attitude.

You choose your attitude in any given set of circumstances. Your attitude is completely independent of circumstances, just as your conscious thought is. When something happens, you have the choice to react through habit or to respond through awareness. The choice is yours.

Your attitude started to form when you were young, even while you were in the womb. While you were an infant, your subconscious mind was wide open to outside influence. You couldn't stop the thoughts, feelings, and actions of those around you from going right into your subconscious and becoming fixed. Pause for a moment and ask yourself: What was the attitude of the people around you when you were an infant. Now realize that you are an extension of that energy to a degree.

Authority figures in your life shaped and molded your attitude to an enormous degree. It is amazing when we stop and think about it. This may be a good thing, and this may be a very bad thing, but either way you are now in a position to change it completely or improve it immensely. Again, reflect upon the authority figures in your early life, and become aware that some of their mental programming is your mental programming. This may seem like a shock at first, but I can assure you it is the truth. I will show you exactly how to change your attitude as you read further in this chapter.

Your own choices formed your attitude as well. We all make choices every single day, and the choices you consistently make form your habits and your attitudes. Every single morning, no matter what happened the day before, you have a choice to set the attitude that you want to embody and hold that vibration throughout the rest of the day. The sooner you make that decision, the better your day will become.

ATTITUDES IMPACT ON FAMILY LIFE

Negative attitudes from you generate negative attitudes toward you, and it can be no other way. Remember, with every feeling and action you are sending out a vibration that everyone around you can *feel*, whether they know it or not. Have you ever walked into a room and just knew something was wrong with someone? He or she didn't say anything to you, but you just felt that something bad had happened to that person that day. Too many people bring home all the baggage they acquire from their workday, and, unfortunately, it is at the expense of their families. Right before you get home from work, decide to adjust your attitude accordingly, and cultivate an attitude of gratitude that you have a family, they are all present, and you have time to spend with them.

If you have an attitude of "have to" do such and such with your family, they will have a "have to" attitude of spending time with you. What you put out comes back, and your actions will be modeled by your children. We have no idea just how big of an impact we have on our children. Not so much as what we say, but by what we do.

I just described how this can work in a negative manner, and it works exactly the same in a positive manner.

Positive attitude from you generates positive attitude toward you. If you have a positive attitude, your family will have a positive attitude toward you. This again is the law of cause and effect manifesting in your life. What you put out will come back to you.

You will have more fun together, and that will perpetuate itself and create more positive circumstances in your family life. It is a beautiful cycle; controlling your attitude will have major benefits. The more you are grateful for the good times, the more good times you will have with your family. It doesn't get any simpler than that, and it doesn't get any better than that.

The better your emotions, the better you communicate. Communication is arguably the most vital aspect in any relationship. The better you are able to communicate to the outside world, the better your life will be. Every single relationship will improve, including the relationship you have with yourself.

The better you communicate, the better all your relationships become. Have you ever tried to carry on a conversation with someone in a very bad mood? It is almost impossible isn't it? The more anger you are harboring, the more altered your perception becomes of your current reality.

ATTITUDES IMPACT ON HEALTH

Your emotions affect your health significantly, more than you can imagine. Every single emotion is like putting something in your body. It is like eating a piece of food—literally. You have experienced this before. Remember when you had a major worry in your life and then you received news that it was all over, and there was nothing to worry about? Did you feel the world was lifted from your shoulders? That is an example of how emotions are literally stored in your body and have significant influence on your health and state of being.

The better your attitude, the better you *feel*; the better you feel, the more efficient your actions; the more efficient your actions, the better your results are. If you want to begin to change your attitude toward yourself in a hurry, start by positively impacting your physical health through exercise or dieting. You will find your attitude instantly improves when you do this.

A negative attitude affects your immune system. It literally lowers your immune system and makes you more susceptible to sickness and disease. Talk to a chiropractor or a healer and that person will tell you some of the main components to sound health are proper movement, nutrition, and positive thoughts.

When you get sick, you will not heal as fast. This may sound slightly erroneous, but many studies have proven that people with positive attitudes heal faster and often produce amazing results with their physical healing.

You will be more susceptible to getting sick, and you will find that your will leads you to ways and means by which you will get sick! Remember, you literally become what you think about. You rarely find someone in a constant negative state who is vibrant and healthy!

The better your attitude, the better you feel, and when you feel good, people can just tell. You can tell when someone is in a positive vibration by the way that person walks, talks, and sounds. Your body will instantly respond to changes in your attitude and feelings.

You will discover that you won't get sick as often, and when you do, you won't stay sick as long.

Pure thoughts cause you not to desire unhealthy food. James Allen said that in his classic book *As a Man Thinketh*. This sounds too good to be true, but the more you feel good, the more you will desire to feel good, and you will not want to put any toxic food into your system. Remember, every emotion perpetuates itself, and your mind will constantly look for ways and means by which to keep manifesting the thoughts you are holding onto; health is no different.

ATTITUDES IMPACT ON SOCIAL LIFE

Have you ever talked to someone with a negative attitude? It probably wasn't very fun. That person probably was not full of jokes, good stories, or wonderful memories. *Who wants to talk with someone like that*!!! Not me, and I'm sure you do not want to either.

People will not want to spend a lot of time with you if you are in a constant negative state. The only people who will want to be with you are other completely negative people, and you will all love to hang around and complain about everything that is wrong in the world and do nothing about it. "Misery loves company" is a very true statement.

Cause and effect. Emmerson called the law of cause and effect the law of laws; it has everything to do with relationships. If you walk into a room with a negative attitude, no one but negative people will gravitate to you. If you are in a positive vibration, then you will instantly have other like minded people gravitate toward you. It is just that simple.

An attractive personality is someone with a positive attitude. Someone with a positive attitude is someone you want to be around, socialize with, and even emulate. What is it about that person? It is nothing more or less than their attitude; that is what makes you interested in the first place.

You will be magnetic, vibrant, and full of life! You will literally be a light for people, and they will be attracted to you. They will know they want to be around you even before they meet you. Why is this? It is your vibration, your attitude.

People will want to be around you and *stay* around you. You will find yourself developing great relationships that are both meaningful and profitable.

People who have never met you before will seek you out to do business with you. There is no better marketing than your own attitude. You can't buy a billboard big enough to cover up a negative attitude.

ATTITUDES IMPACT ON FINANCIAL LIFE

It has everything to do with money. My original mentor Bob Proctor told me that money can't talk, but it can hear, and if you call it, it will come. How do you call it? It starts with your attitude. Get out and get in massive action with the right thoughts, feelings, and actions, and you will find that money will chase you down and follow you.

If you have a negative attitude toward a friend, is that person your friend long? It is the same with money; you will literally repel it. When you suddenly acquire a large amount of it, you will automatically self defeat and spend it or lose it. Why? Because you will become what you think about. If you think bad thoughts toward money, you are telling the universe that you don't want any of it, and the universe says your wish is my command.

Negative attitude equals poor service, and poor service does not produce lasting wealth. The greatest among you is the servant, and the wealthiest among you is the servant. Bottom line.

Money will avoid you, escape you, and be a constant source of frustration for you the more you maintain and perpetuate a negative attitude toward it.

Having a positive attitude toward it, you will attract more money, and it will come to you more consistently because your actions will be consistent.

You will provide better service, and better service is one of the aspects to the law of compensation that I will discuss later in the chapter on earning more money. You will want to read ahead for that one!

People will want to do business with you, and they will literally seek you out, just as I stated earlier. This all sounds crazy until you experience it; then it gets even crazier!

How to Improve Your Attitude

It starts today! It starts the minute you decide it is going to improve. *Know this*: Every single morning you must come back to the decision and to the commitment that you are holding a positive attitude all day long, no matter what. Lock into that vibration, and the universe will reinvent itself to bring you good things; it is pure unadulterated magic!

Step 1: Describe the attitude you want in every detail possible. When you have a circumstance where your attitude gets sidetracked, write exactly how you want your attitude to be relative to that circumstance. *You do not describe what you embody; you embody what you describe.* Describe your attitude.

Step 2: Read it every day. Every single morning and every single night as a reminder to the attitude you are holding, and make sure your children see this description.

Step 3: Get around the right people ASAP! Once you have decided you are changing your life, I want to know, and I want to connect you with the right people, the right family, and the right vehicle that will take you from where you are to where you want and *deserve* to be!

2

WORKING WITH
THE LAW

"*All of the great achievers of the past have been
visionary figures; they were men and women
who projected into the future. They thought of
what could be, rather than what already was,
and then they moved themselves into action, to
bring these things into fruition.*"

–Bob Proctor

BE, DO, HAVE

It is more important to *be*. The ability to *be* is more important than doing or having. To *have* the things you desire, you will need to *do* actions in a certain way.

You can *be* anything! It is vital to your success to *be*. Imagine what you desire and what it will feel like to actually have it!

If you sincerely desire to *do* the actions you must take to *have* what you desire from life, figure out and assume the correct *be*. I recommend you take these steps.

- Write down something you desire to *have*.

- Write the action steps you need to *do* to get what you desire.

- Use your imagination to figure out the identity you must *be*. Write down the characteristics, qualities and the features of this identity.

- Assume the correct identity of the characteristics before starting the actions.

- When you are being what you need to *be*, you will be very excited to start the *do*. Just *do* it!

- You must believe what is true to you, to be true to you! You must ignore those who criticize you for being what you need to *be* or doing what you need to *do* to get what you want to *have* from your life. Check this out: When you reach your goals, the small minded people will be jealous of your success.

What are you going to *be*? You are meant to have an amazing life! You are meant to live the life of your dreams. You are meant to have all that you love and desire. You have the power inside of you to manifest in the natural, everything you love to be, do, or have.

Whatever you desire in life, you desire because you love it. Love is the most powerful force in the universe. Everything you want to be, do, or have comes from love. Think and talk about what you love more than what you don't love.

Although you can have whatever you love and want, you must harmonize with love. You will not get what you want unless you give love. Criticizing, blaming, finding faults in others, and complaining will prevent you from having the amazing life you desire.

The mighty force of *love* is the intelligence of life and the universe. Never put anything above love. Love must be the ruling force in your life! Now this powerful love will do anything for you, but the only way to unite with it is through love. So welcome love into your life as your personal assistant and money manager!

Once you are living the love walk, you can attract your desires to you on purpose. Remember to imagine it, feel it, and receive it! Your job in the creation process is to imagine and feel it.

• Imagine using your mind to focus on and image what you desire. Picture yourself being with your desire, doing things you desire, and having your desire. Desire is love!

• Feel it at the same time you imagine it. You must feel love for what you are imagining. Image and feel being with what you desire. Image and feel doing things with your desire.

Your imagination connects you to what you love. I'm going to show you how powerful you are. Once you are having a burning desire and feeling it, you have created the magnetism. The magnetic power attracts your desire to you.

Receive it! Whatever you want to be, do, or have in life, the creation process is the same. The force of love will be working through the invisible and visible forces to bring you what you desire.

Your entire life is what you have imagined it to be!

---

*Then you will know the truth
and the truth will set you free.*

—Jesus (John 8:32)

HOW TO BE WHAT YOU WANT TO BE

You have the capacity to be, do, and have whatever your heart desires. You must recognize the power within is God, and consciously identify yourself with God. We all have been given a specific purpose for our life, and only you can discover your purpose. This Earth operates by natural laws. These laws are operating in your life whether or not you know it.

You may see God as Love, Universe, Divine Mind, Lord, Jehovah, Divine Intelligence, or other names you choose. They mean one and the same thing. I have learned to call God working in my life, *law*.

As we strive to harmonize our life with the laws governing the universe, we are consciously living closer to God, which brings us a better understanding. He is as close to us as the breath we breathe.

We are involved deeply in a mind (God, universe) that knows all, and that mind contains all knowledge and all truth. It is seeking to give us this knowledge. This limitless wisdom and power are open to everyone. You can draw from it as you will and according to your needs.

Remember, you can make yourself what you desire to *be*; you can do what you wish to *do*; you can *have* what you want. If you really desire to *be*, *do*, and *have* all that your heart desires, you must become aware of your oneness with God. Thus, you may perceive truth, have wisdom, and know the right ends to seek and the right means to use to attain those ends, and of course, so that you may secure power and ability to use the means.

In the history of the human race, all the great leaders have disagreed on many thing, but they all agreed that our power, possibility, and promise lie in our mind. We become what we think about.

Our mind is the creative cause of all that happens in our life. Before we ever make a move of any kind, we first form some image or plan in the mind. Results in your life are the direct outcome of your ideas.

You have the power to control your circumstances; by using this power, you can create other circumstances to gain your desires at a higher nature.

All things are possible in spirit. Spirit is a sensitive, unseen, creative substance in its original state, with the sole purpose of expansion and fuller expression. Once you fully understand this great truth, it will become the most important consideration for you. Once you become aware of the truth, the character with which this sensitive, reproductive power is invested, you will know the Universal Creative Power can be only what you feel and think it to be. If you think your thoughts are powerful, your thoughts are powerful, and spirit will become an eagle and willing to help you.

KEY TO SUCCESS IN LIVING LIFE

You must first understand how your mind functions. Mind is movement. The conscious mind is the part of you that thinks and reasons; it's where your free will lies. The conscious mind can accept or reject any idea. As you accept a thought, it is impressed upon the second part of your personality.

The second part is the subconscious mind, the power center, where your emotions lie. It is how you connect with the infinite. It is the God part of you also known as spirit. It knows no limits. Whatever thought your conscious mind chooses to accept, it has no ability to reject. It does not know the difference between what is real and what is imagined. This part of you operates in an orderly manner. Any thought repeatedly impressed on your subconscious mind will become habit. By natural law, it expresses itself through you, in feelings and actions.

Most people are constantly thinking about what they do not want. They are unconsciously sending negative vibrations into the universe, and, of course, the universe gives them more negative situations.

By law, the more we focus on that which we do not want or like, the more we will attract it into our lives. We must learn to persevere, focus only on the good in everything, and be in a constant state of gratitude, regardless of circumstances. We need to learn, to shift from a state of negativity to a position of gratitude and faith.

The source and cause of all success are hidden deep within your mind. Thus, if you believe in honesty, you will support the principle of honesty. If you are given the opportunity to cheat or steal from someone, you will hold the principle of honesty firmly and refuse to take advantage of someone. This mean you are charging your mind with honesty, and it becomes magnetic to attract honesty endeavors and permanent success.

IDEAS DETERMINE THE CONDITION IN YOUR LIFE

An idea is a thought or a group of thoughts. An idea is an image or a picture in the mind. All conditions are the result of our actions, and all actions are the outcome of our ideas. Our ideas determine the conditions in our daily lives.

We are constantly thinking. We can change our thoughts, but we cannot stop thinking. Thinking is power that is flowing in and through us like the air we breathe. I like to refer to this power as spirit or energy. If we are not consciously and on purpose giving it direction, then other people and circumstances, the outside world, are going to give it direction. That is where confusion takes over and produces confused results.

GETTING YOUR PRAYERS ANSWERED

Prayer is simply total concentration on a subject at hand. We use prayer to quiet our mental state, which raises the level of our mental vibrations. When you are in total concentration, the levels of your mental vibration rise, helping you to attract to you what you are asking for.

Prayer is an appeal to a higher authority power—God! It is asking for some type of an event to take place. The majority of time, prayer is for healing, wisdom, health, or wealth for ourselves or someone else.

Prayer is the common doorway to the spiritual realm.

The nonphysical level of life is always moving into physical form. The physical level of life is the manifestation of the nonphysical. Prayer is the movement that takes place between spirit and form with and through you.

I have come to realize when I pray for one thing and then fear and doubt that I will receive it, I then scatter my mental forces and can only attract what my lesser thoughts believe and expect.

Everyone is governed by the same laws whether you know it or not. Many people blame God when they do not get the answer they were seeking. They use God as their excuse when they are unable to explain some act of nature.

You must realize it is only your fault if your prayers are left unanswered. The creative law is always ready to answer and cannot fail to respond when approached rightly and wisely.

CREATIVE POWER OF YOUR MIND

There is a scientific way of thinking about everything, a true and right way, which will prevent needless waste of mental energy and produce the desired results. All things and events, all experiences and conditions of life are results.

f

Thomas Troward stated, "It's an old saying that Order is Heaven's First Law and like many other old sayings it contains a much deeper philosophy than appears immediately on the surface."

Getting things into a better order is the great secret of progress; we are now able to fly through the air, not because the laws of nature have altered, but because we have learned to arrange things in the right order to produce this result. The things themselves had existed from the beginning of the world, but what was lacking was the introduction of a personal factor that, by an intelligent perception of the possibilities contained in the laws of nature, would be able to bring into working reality ideas that previous generations would have laughed at as the absurd fancies of an unbalanced mind.

The lesson to be learned from the practical aviation of the present day is that of the triumph of principle over precedent, of the working out of an idea to its logical conclusions in spite of the accumulated testimony of all past experience to the contrary. With such a notable example before us, can we say that it is futile to inquire whether by the same method we may not unlock still more important secrets and gain some knowledge of the unseen causes that are at the back of external and visible conditions and then, by bringing these unseen causes into a better order, make practical working realities of possibilities that at present seem but fantastic dreams.

CREATE YOUR GOOD LIFE

Life with all attributes of good is something that doesn't just happen. It is something you must create. It is something you must plan, picture mentally, and think about. You cannot find, buy, or borrow from anyone else, when you are seeking love, fortune, happiness, and success. No one can give it to you; you must create it within yourself. Your desires and ideas are like seeds you plant, but they are planted in the soil of the mind. You must cultivate, nurture, and guard your thought seeds until the harvest time. Then you will abundantly reap all that you have sown.

We have power; the universal power of mind is endowed within all of us. All that we may ever desire to have and to be is ours for the asking. The power within you is superior to any condition or circumstance around you. When a circumstance arises, we are not to come under it but we are to overcome and master it. No person or circumstance can cause you to think about thoughts or ideas you do not choose. With free will, your thoughts direct the power to whatever results you choose. When exercising the creative law of thinking, you will grow in wisdom and power.

LAW OF THINKING

" *Mind is the great lever of all things;*
human thought is the process by which
human ends are ultimately answered.

–Daniel Webster, 1825 "

LAW OF THINKING

"As a man thinketh in his heart, so is he" (Proverbs 23:7). This is one of the most important laws that we are going to understand and then apply. Your attention should be given to the predominant mental state. This is the foundation of your life. It's the first step to freedom.

We are programmed genetically and environmentally; we have become the product of somebody else's habitual way of thinking. When we were young kids, our subconscious mind was undeveloped. The ideas, thoughts, and images of our parents, teachers, and other authority figures were impressed upon the subconscious part of our mind.

The mind is the basic factor and governing power in the human race. Until we get to the point where we start to understand our mind, we truly do not have control over our life. But it is actually simple. Until we really understand, life will be a deep mystery. Mystery is just another word for ignorance. All things are mysteries when they are not understood.

When you clearly understand how to think properly, it opens the door to freedom. Begin to pay attention to what you are thinking. As your level of awareness is raised, you will notice what you are thinking, and what you predominantly focus on begins to manifest and show itself in your everyday life. Your life will no longer be a mystery.

Thinking is done in our intellectual mind, which is our conscious mind. I want you truly to understand how your mind functions, so I will briefly explain the six intellectual faculties.

Perception: Our perception is our point of view. When we see something that causes us to think something cannot be done, we can change our perception of the situation and originate an idea on how it can be done.

Memory: Our memory is perfect. There is no such thing as a bad memory. There are only weak memories and strong memories. There are exercises you can do to strengthen your memory.

Reason: Reason is what gives us the ability to think. Thinking is our highest function. It is our inductive reasoning faculty that gives us the ability to originate individual thoughts and bring them together in the formation of ideas.

Will: Will gives you the ability to focus and concentrate. It gives you the ability to hold one picture on the screen of your mind to the exclusion of all outside distractions. The more you practice developing your will, the stronger it will become.

Your power lies in being able to decide what you will think about and how you will think. In other words, the function of the will is to direct your thoughts.

Intuition: With your intuition you pick up vibrations and translate those vibrations in your mind. Your intuition permits you to know that you know what is happening around you. I've grown to learn, prayer is us talking to God; intuition is God talking to us.

Imagination: Imagination creates fantasies. Fantasy is the first stage of creation in life. The creative process spans three stages: fantasy, theory, and fact. It is important to remember that without the aid of your imagination, there could be no creation in your life.

f

When we learn to use our mind for advancement, we are using correctly these hidden powers, forces, and faculties. This is the key to success in living life.

TRUTH ABOUT YOUR SENSES

"Seeing is believing" is a phrase that appears to be real to many people. Evidences of the senses are the only fact that some accept. But we must realize that it is what we believe that determines what we shall see.

Our senses—see, hear, smell, taste, and touch—are connected to our conscious mind. Everything in the universe that we can see, hear, smell, taste, or touch, together with our emotions, is the manifestation of energy in various levels of vibration.

Since we are born into a physical body and correspond with a material world, we are programmed to live through our physical five senses. Our senses were given to us to correspond and communicate, keeping us in touch with the outside world.

Spiritual, intellectual, and physical: We are simultaneously living on all three planes of being. An ignorant person permits the appearance of things to control his or her thoughts.

There is much more to yourself than you can see, and you must comprehend this hidden factor of your personality, that is, if you are ever to develop yourself properly. The truth is, you will never see the greatest part of your being. It is nonphysical in nature.

You must become aware that you are constantly living on three distinct planes of being.

You are spiritual. You have an intellect. You live in a physical body.

1. Spiritual: nonphysical/thought/energy

2. Intellectual: ideas

3. Physical: things or results

All you can possibly need or desire is already yours.
Call your desires into being by imagining
and feeling your wish fulfilled.

-Neville Goddard (1905–1972)

VISUALIZATION

Visualizing is the ability of your mind to see things in pictures. When you visualize, you are allowing yourself to see things you want. The secret is being able to hold the goal long enough to produce a clear picture of it. View your picture as reality. Before long you will see what you visualized.

When you visualize something, you are visualizing something you have already experienced that is already impressed into your brain cells. Any time you recall an experience of any kind, you are visualizing.

Visualization is recalling and replaying memories that involve each of your sensory functions.

Imagination is creating something for the first time. The moment you have already created it and you recall it, that is visualization.

Do not confuse visualization with daydreaming either. Visualization is an act of the will that enables you through focus and concentration to create a mental image of yourself and what you desire.

MANIFESTATION

Many people have a false belief of what manifesting is. They think manifesting is creating something out of nothing. I'm going to let you in on a little secret. Manifestation is simply becoming aware of what already exists. Yes, it is just that simple!

Have you ever believed and expected something that you did not receive no matter how hard you envisioned your dream? I know you may say I believed, expected, and envisioned my dream manifesting, I've done everything, and my dream still hasn't manifested. To tell you the truth, you are resisting doing something.

Take a moment, and I want you to really think. Be true to yourself! Have you ever had an idea that you totally dismissed? You probably dismissed it because it made you uncomfortable. In the back of your mind, you know you should be doing it. You do not act on the idea because the action is pushing you past your comfort zone; staying where you are is protecting something inside you in some way. You are unconsciously thinking you need to protect yourself. Because you are thinking this way, you have impressed those thoughts upon your subconscious mind. That is the reason for the resistance.

Suppose you would like to earn $20,000 a month so that your family will live comfortably, not having to worry about paying bills. You know earning this sum of money monthly would make a big difference. However, you do not know how to earn $20,000 a month. The way to earn the money is already present; it's that you are not aware how to earn it.

If you ask the universe how and listen to your inner thoughts, the answer will be apparent. You dismiss the ideas because it's forcing you to face your fears: like having to ask someone to buy from you. You may think, I do not want to deal with rejections: like having to speak in front of others; you think, I hate speaking in front of a group.

So you do not manifest or become aware of what you desire. Remember what you resist will persist. Not manifesting the $20,000 a month that you really need is keeping your family struggling.

How Greatness Is Attained

Greatness is attained only by constantly thinking great thoughts. You cannot become great in your outward personality until you are great internally. You cannot become great internally until you begin to think properly. No amount of formal education, study, or reading can make you great without thought, but your thoughts can make you great with very little study. You are mentally developed by what you think about what you read, not by what you read.

From my intense thoughts after reading Wallace D. Wattles' books, I have come to believe universal spirit is the intelligent substance from which all things come; it is in and through all things. This is powerful! All things are known to this universal mind, and you can unite yourself with it. You will then enter into all knowledge.

Greatness is inherent in everyone, and may be manifested by all. Everyone may become great. If you desire to become great, the soul must act and must rule the mind and body. Our knowledge is limited; we fall into error through ignorance. If you desire to avoid this error, you must connect your soul with universal spirit.

So, you want to understand how to stay connected to this power? You must cast out everything that separates you from God, like jealousy, envy, strife, gossip, and being hateful. You must will to live divine life and rise above all moral temptations. You must forsake all courses of action that are not aligned with your highest ideals.

You must form a mental conception of yourself at the highest, and hold the conception until it is your habitual thought-form. You must outwardly realize and express your thought-form in your actions. You must do everything you do in a great way. That includes dealing with your family, friends, neighbors, and acquaintances; every act must be an expression of your ideals. You will then make yourself known and be recognized as a personality of power. You will receive knowledge by inspiration and will know all that you need to know. You will receive all material wealth you form in your thoughts. You will not lack for any good thing. Great works will seek you out, and all will be delighted to honor you. Wow!

> *Through your ability to think and feel,*
> *you have dominion over all creation.*
>
> –Neville Goddard (1905–1972)

YOUR INFINITE POWER

To walk in your infinite power, you must understand there's a cosmic intelligence which is in all things and through all things. This is the one real substance: original source. From this source all things proceed; it is intelligent substance or mind stuff. You guessed it! God is all, in all, and there is nothing wrong.

All men and women everywhere are good and perfect. All is right with the world. We are here on earth to unite with God for the completion of the perfect work. We all have a special gift. We all are unique. It is only as you see God as the Great Advancing Presence in all and good in all, that you can rise to real greatness. Truly walking in your power.

We must recognize that we are one with God our Father. We must become consciously aware of our oneness. You must know that you are a god among other gods, and act accordingly. You must have absolute faith in your own perceptions of truth. You must cease to act unthinkingly, and begin to think and be sincere in your thoughts.

Thought is in the spirit substance which is the real you. You think and express your thoughts through your brain. The spirit substance of us spiritual beings permeates the body, thinks, and knows in the body. Thus, the Original Spirit Substance, God, permeates all nature, thinks, and knows in nature. Nature is as intelligent as all of us. Nature knows more than we know; nature knows all things. The All Mind, God, has been in touch with all things from the beginning and contains all knowledge.

All that is and all that has been are equally present everywhere. We are a thinking substance. All intelligence, power, and force come from cosmic substance, God our Father. When you consciously become aware to unite all your wisdom and power with cosmic intelligence, you will perceive the thoughts of God. You then have become aware of your oneness with spirit, which is the foundation of your knowledge and power.

God is spirit. We are spiritual beings. Become spiritually awakened, and you will see His kingdom. I'm talking Heaven on Earth!

When you are living in God's kingdom on Earth, you will rely on and believe in your unlimited potential and power, having no anxiety about financial or any other matters. Because you know God, who is within you, is also in all things you want. All your trust will be placed in God.

When you are spiritually awakened, God will give you all power.

4

LAW OF BELIEF

You block your dream when you allow your fear to grow bigger than your faith.

—Mary Manin Morrissey

WHAT BELIEF ACTUALLY IS

A belief is an idea that I am convinced about. This belief may have originated from a book I once read, an experience I had, or even from a memory that keeps playing over and over in my mind. A belief goes beyond thinking something is true; it is a deep seated knowing.

A belief is something I know that I know.

A belief may be true, or it may be totally incorrect. A belief can be good and bad.

If I believe in negative things, then the belief turns against me; if my belief is channeled positively, then I will rise to the height of that belief. This may be slightly confusing in the beginning, but as you read through this chapter, you will walk into an understanding and be able to take appropriate action.

Learning about my beliefs and their power over my actions has absolutely transformed my life. I see many people attempting to achieve results that are completely contrary to their belief system. Thus, failure and heartache always find them. For example, if you are trying to earn more money and one of your *hidden* beliefs is that you are not worthy of money, you will always find yourself wanting. You will go through valleys and peaks, but always end up with not enough due to the simple truth that you attract what is in harmony with your beliefs. "All things can be done for the one who believes" is a statement of power if your beliefs are positive, but it can just as easily turn into a statement of pain if you are not able to channel your beliefs away from negativity.

You can only change that which you are consciously aware of. And our beliefs are contained in our subconscious mind and stay out of our conscious gaze unless we start to contemplate and really "go within" to discover what those beliefs are. When you can consciously realize what your beliefs are, then you can rid yourself of the negative ones and expand the positive beliefs. Nothing becomes real to you until you are aware that it is real.

How Belief Can Be Positive and Negative

Beliefs can be negative if they are not based on truth. Just because you believe something does not make it true. Ask yourself: Is that true, or is that what you believe? That is a powerful question to ask yourself whenever you realize a belief needs changing.

If you believe you are a total failure, then that is exactly what will manifest in your life. Now, is that belief true? *Absolutely not.* God doesn't make failures. But again, all things can be done for the one who believes. The entire universe will bend and mold itself to help your beliefs manifest themselves. That is what the universe was made for.

Beliefs can be tremendously positive if they are based on truth.

You will rise only as far as your beliefs will let you; there truly are no limits.

Beliefs are very good if they promote your potential. I believe emotions and beliefs are what channel your potential and give it the direction it needs to manifest. They are the gateway to your highest self.

Your beliefs will unlock your inner genius. Every single person is a genius in some way, shape, or form. I so truly and completely believe in this that I have committed my entire life's work to help people be introduced to their own inner genius. You—*yes you*—are an absolute complete and total genius.

ʃ

I may not know you; I may not know anything about your past, or how you want your future to go. But I do know one thing: that all human beings were created with exactly the same potential. When you look at someone in the eye, you are looking at a mirror reflection of yourself.

We are all one. *No one* has any more potential than anyone else. Your creator is fair.

How to Be a More Positive and Optimistic Person

Positivity and optimism are also beliefs. How do you become this person? First, you must know in your heart that you can resolve the challenge no matter what happens, knowing it will not get you down. You must be able to respond in a constructive way. When you consciously make a decision, you prepare yourself mentally if things do not go well, which they may not, and you will not be knocked off balance.

Make all your negative thoughts ineffective by always speaking to yourself in a positive manner. You can repeat affirmations like, *I am* so happy and grateful I have a loving family, *I am* so happy and grateful I'm healthy, *I am* so happy and grateful I'm alive and full of joy, *I am* so happy and grateful that I understand how to love myself. Remember whatever you expressed is impressed upon the subconscious mind, the God like part of you! As thoughts are impressed upon your subconscious mind, they will become your personality.

Look at each challenge and setback as being only temporary external force. See each negative situation as not being connected to any other future events. See them as being caused by an external factor, over which you have little control. For example, you purchased a home three years old ago valued at $500,000; due to the economy in the real estate market, your home is now valued at $250,000. You must refuse to see the negative situation as a permanent inability. To help calm your mind say, God (or whomever you see as your Higher Power), thank you for granting me the serenity to accept things I cannot change, the courage to change the things I can, and the wisdom to know the difference.

}

As you learn and grow successfully, you will have adversities. You must be able to strive and rise above them to become a better person. Keep your thoughts on the perfect outcome of every situation.

If you need to search for peace of mind, ask God. Be sure that you release all negative energy. Surrender yourself to the place of peace. Being loving to others no matter what will cast fear— "False Evidence Appearing Real"—out of your life; it will help bring you peace of mind. Know that the challenge is not the challenge but your thinking of the challenge.

When you bring yourself to a place of peace, you bring yourself to a place of no thoughts. You may have heard it called the place of presence. Have faith your Higher Power will guide you and reveal answers even if you do not see it in the natural yet. Completely surrender yourself by letting go of the situation and letting God in. Say out loud, peace be still!

God always operates in a very exact way! This is what we refer to as laws of nature, what I'm speaking about throughout *Walk in Your Power*. When we can truly turn the challenge over to God, who is within us, we will move into a new vibration. Then watch how the challenging situation changes. You will act differently and attract differently. Then expect a big gift from God: abundance.

How Belief Strengthens Us

Your motivation is based on your belief of whether or not you will be successful. Why would you be motivated to do something you believe will end in failure?

When you wake up in the morning, if you believe bad things are going to happen, you will not want to get out of bed! Start to affirm the success of what is to come in your life. Take ownership, and claim the things you want in your life before they arrive. Feel good!

You will be much more committed if you believe you will succeed. You will not hesitate; you will not hold back. And other people will sense your belief and your commitment immediately, and they will want to join you in your cause.

Do everything in a great way, and you will find your beliefs will make you unstoppable.

HOW TO STRENGTHEN YOUR BELIEFS

The first step is to stop listening to negative media. You can read or hear a lie over and over and eventually believe it.

Stop talking to negative people. Why? Because they are negative! You will become the people you hang around. Get around some positive people who are getting much better results than you are. They will raise your vibration and strengthen your beliefs. Your mind and habits will mold to match theirs.

Listen to personal development programs repeatedly. I'm absolutely obsessed with these programs. Play them often, and listen to them even when you cannot give them your full attention. Have them playing subliminally in the background while working. Even though you cannot consciously listen to every word, your subconscious mind will be receiving benefit through the power of autosuggestion.

Repetition is the first law of learning on any subject. You have formed your beliefs by repeatedly entertaining some form of thought and action. You read it, heard it, and affirmed it over and over again. That is exactly how you can change your beliefs to be positive. Affirm them, speak them, write about them, and you will be living them!

YOUR SELF TALK

Your internal conversations that you have in your mind are what constitute your self talk. Everyone talks to themselves whether or not we want to admit it. We are all constantly having conversations with ourselves—as weird as it sounds.

Be aware of your self talk throughout the day. Pay attention to what you are saying to yourself. When you drop something, what are you saying out loud or silently in your mind? When you receive a compliment from someone else, what are you saying to yourself? Do you affirm it and agree with it, or do you silently reject the compliment? These are powerful things to be doing.

If your self talk is negative, it will depower you and drain you of all energy. We have a tendency rarely to think well of ourselves. What I am revealing to you right now has the power to transform your life completely and instantly make you feel better about yourself.

If your self talk is positive, it will empower you. If you are constantly affirming to yourself that you are a great person, you are a winner, you are a powerful being, you will feel better. If someone compliments you, show them appreciation, and silently in your own mind affirm that and agree with it, your self image will constantly be improving. When you drop something or make a mistake, don't beat yourself up about it. Instead, just say this: "That isn't like me." Saying that will completely separate you from the unwanted action, and you will rarely partake in it again.

Your self talk builds your beliefs or tears them down. You know that you become what you think about, and paying attention to your self talk reveals a great deal regarding your constant thoughts.

Your self talk identifies what your beliefs are. If you find you self talk to be degrading and negative, then you know you have some beliefs to change regarding how you see yourself. Hear the negative self talk, and reverse it to say the exact opposite.

CHANGE YOUR NEGATIVE PROGRAMMING

You may not be in love with yourself and desire to change your life, but you are not sure how to change your life to make a difference. I can tell you this: If you continue to think what you always thought, you will keep getting what you always got.

f

There are many people who have no clue how they got what they have in life. They think life is just happening to them. Well, life does not happen to you; life is happening because of you. Those people are not realizing they are attracting the lack, struggles, and unhappiness because they are not using or applying the fixed scientific laws of the universe appropriately. No problem; I have your back! This book is revealing what the laws are and how to apply them on purpose. You are guaranteed to be happy and prosperous when you understand, master, and apply the fixed scientific laws.

CHANGE LIMITED BELIEFS

In order to change your limited beliefs, you must first understand how you learned the belief. Beliefs are a habitual way of thinking. When you have thoughts you constantly think about or affirmations you repeat to yourself or someone else repeat to you, they become your habitual way of thinking. Know that your happiness, success, or fortune will never exceed the size of your beliefs. To create new beliefs, you will do the same process you did to create the old beliefs: a habitual way of thinking, but this time you will consciously focus on what you desire.

THE POWER OF AFFIRMATIONS

A positive statement to yourself, from yourself, is what an affirmation essentially is. You are making a declaration of a future state of being you want to experience. If you want wealth in your life, you would make an affirmation regarding how wealthy you are. Even if the wealth isn't there now, create an affirmation that is something similar to: "I am bursting with joy, peace, gratitude, *and money!*" and say it over and over and over. You become what you think about. Right?

So make an affirmation and think about it *all the time*!

An affirmation gives direction to your repeated self talk. An affirmation tells your mind what you want to be thinking about. An affirmation tells the universe who you are, what you want, and declares your *"beingness."*

The purpose of an affirmation is to take control of your self talk and of your consciousness. You are the only creature on the planet that we are aware of that can claim the description "sentient being," meaning "consciously aware." You can direct the most powerful substance on planet Earth—energy. If you can master your self talk through affirmations, you can be the master of energy and direct it to manifest whatever you want.

You become what you think about all day long. So create an affirmation that states exactly how you want to live, and think on it over and over and over and over again!

Have it start with "I am." The words "I am" are the two most powerful words a human being can utter. As soon as you say those two words, unlimited energy flows right into your consciousness, and when it first enters your mind, it has no form. Whatever you say after "I am" is the form that energy is going to take. We are constantly making "I am" statements all day. "I am" tired, "I am" really not looking forward to this meeting, "I am" excited for the party tonight, and so forth. If you pay attention to your "I am" statements, you will be aware that they are in perfect alignment with your results. "I am." They are the two words correlated with all creation.

It should be emotionally appealing. Your affirmation takes on a great power according to your emotional involvement with it. The more emotionally appealing, the more powerful the affirmation. Make it beautiful and big!

Your results in life are outward expressions of your paradigm. They house your inner belief system. In an effort to understand your various beliefs, you must first examine your results.

Focus and clearly describe results you are getting in these areas:

- Your relationships
- Your physical health
- Your finances
- The contributions you are giving to your community

Thomas Troward stated, "Whatsoever not of faith" that is not in accordance with our honest belief "is sin," and by acting contrary to what we really believe, we bring in a suggestion of opposition to the Divine Spirit that must necessarily paralyze our efforts and surround us with a murky atmosphere of distrust and want of joy.

But all this exists in and is produced by our belief, and when we come to examine the grounds of this belief, we shall find that it rests upon an entire misapprehension of the nature of our own power.

5

LAW OF NONRESISTANCE

Nonresistance is the key to the greatest power in the Universe.

–Eckhart Tolle

WHATEVER YOU RESIST WILL PERSIST.

The law of nonresistance will bring absolute freedom in your life.

All of us have had some sort of ideas that are products of mass thinking and have been implanted in us, such as "This is too good to be true" or "I don't think this will last." Start to recognize some of the ideas and patterns that create resistance that you may still be using.

Notice when you are holding thoughts that are actually resisting the greater good that would flow naturally into your life. As you understand the law of nonresistance, you will see how there is something powerful in the idea of releasing the resistance that you may have to gain the good that is your birthright.

Let's say you are in a very busy grocery store in line to pay for your items. You are waiting in a long line; you begin to complain: Someone needs to open another line; the cashier needs to move faster. Well, you are resisting what *is*.

You could easily direct your mind by thinking thoughts like: This store has great prices; this store has good customer service. You could talk to someone that is standing in line with you by speaking positively and cheerfully to raise their vibration. You can relax your mind by thinking about your desires. This is being nonresistant to the situation.

Throughout life, we have been conditioned in our genetic makeup and environment to react to a situation. Reacting is a habit. So when a bad situation arises, most people will react to it, fight it, and resist it. Reacting is an automatic response without giving any conscious thought.

Responding to a situation we will have to think; therefore, nonresistance is not from our conditioning. We are conditioned to resist because we are conditioned to react.

The law of resistance does not require us to work against things we do not want. It requires us to work with and for that which we do want.

We should not be giving our time, energy, or thought to what is opposed to what we want. When you give your time, your energy, or your thoughts to something that is opposed to what you desire, you are actually setting up a resistance that is contrary to the law. That resistance is getting in the way of the good that is coming to you.

We say: I want fulfillment; I want success; I desire an increase of material wealth. But we don't realize when we agree with difficult conditions, like talking about how someone else got ahead and how unfair it is, or any type of energy that is lower in nature or not in harmony with the thing we say we want, we are actually creating resistance to the thing we want. So you ask, how do we experience the greater flow to us? By being nonresistant, by being in agreement with all that is prosperous.

Many of us create our own obstacles to success. We set up everything we need to succeed. At the last moment, we tend to sabotage ourselves by creating resistance. Speaking of poverty and discord, we stop the flow of the good that is coming to us. Therefore, stop working on getting rid of your thoughts of limitation, and focus on increasing your thoughts of prosperity.

OVERCOMING OBSTACLES

I've learned through trials and errors that obstacles are opportunities.

We all are on this earth, life is happening, and some of the obstacles we face are very scary. Consciously, a part of our mind tells us we will not make it, but deep down we know we will make it through. Eventually, we will make it through and move to bigger and better obstacles.

To tell you the truth, obstacles are typically self imposed, nothing more than an illusion. Of course, when we are facing the obstacles, they appear huge. Obstacles of life are placed in our path as an opportunity to raise our level of consciousness. As you become more aware, you will notice the beautiful blessing that was there along the way.

No matter what obstacles may lie ahead of you, you must realize you have the ability to change what you are thinking. Remove the fear by turning it into faith. Just know this: If you do not have obstacles, you are not growing. The only people that do not have obstacles are dead. Life consists of continual obstacles, small and large. It doesn't matter how smart and clever you are, you will face challenges.

What's really important is the growth you experience as you overcome the challenges. As you are moving along in your journey, know that you have the power inside of you eagerly waiting to surface. So start taking advance of the obstacles you are faced with because you know once you solve the problem you will be a bigger and better person.

When you are faced with an obstacle simply relax, so that you may clear your mind. Place yourself in a calm and cool state of mind, so that you may gain control of your emotions and senses. With a certain amount of detachment, become objective, and look at the situation as though it were happening to someone else.

If it appears something is blocking your process of what you are attempting to achieve, I know it is human nature to focus on the problem because "it" is considered important. If you focus on the problem, you are just feeding the obstacle; therefore, the obstacle grows.

As I say throughout the book, focus only on what you want, not what you do not want; believe what you want already exists, because it does! By taking one step at a time, move toward it in faith.

That truly is the secret to manifesting your dreams.

Do the things you are destined to do; the obstacles in your way are you and only you. Personal development growth will help you to conquer the obstacles. Of course, you must be willing to do what it takes to grow wiser.

You will really find out what you are made of when things go wrong and you experience a setback or some form of adversity. Your behavior on the outside is an indicator of who you are on the inside. When you observe your behavior when things go wrong, you will know what you have inside of you. You are only as free as your well developed alternatives and options. If you have not taken the time beforehand to develop alternatives by raising your level of consciousness through personal and/ or business development, you will become anxious and panic when you are suddenly faced with obstacles, adversity, or loss in a particular area of your life.

When you are able to analyze the adversity clearly, sometimes you can see opportunities where you can turn the adversity to your advantage.

Successful people have challenges; the only difference is they respond quickly and positively to their challenges. They think them through in advance; in other words they are proactive. They clearly define the challenges they are facing. They define the worst situation that could happen because of the challenge. They are prepared to deal successfully with the worst should it occur. And they concentrate all their energies on their desired outcome. Many challenges and adversities occur because of incorrect information that leads to misunderstandings. So when you are faced with challenges, say, "This too shall pass." Ask yourself who else may have had the same challenge, and what did that person do? If you know you need help, do not be afraid to ask for help.

That is what we are on earth for: to help one another!

When you are asking yourself questions, did you know you are keeping your mind cool, calm, and objective? You are actually expanding the range of possibilities that are open to you—yours for the asking!

f

Through meditation and our mental faculties, we can seek information and answers to our questions, wherever they may be. It does not matter where the information resides; we have the power to access it, bring it back, and apply it toward solving the challenge.

As your level of spirituality rises, you will be able to use your spiritual senses to seek creative information to solve any challenge. I know by now in your life you have some sense of information that did not solve the problem and some information that did. You have a certain feeling behind each of those situations. Begin to notice how you feel after each one, so that you may ascertain the difference. If you have a thought to do something, do it. It may be the universe guiding you. For example, if you have a thought to read a particular book, read it. You may have a thought to phone a particular person; contact that person. When you have a sincere desire to solve a problem, the answers will come to you. You will solve it!

No More Pain

So you want to know how to create no more pain in your life? Well, nobody's life is completely free of pain and sorrow. You must learn to live with them rather than trying to avoid them.

A lot of the pain and sorrow in our life we bring upon ourselves. When we are not spiritually awakened, a lot of the hurt will be unnecessary self created unconsciously.

The pain you create is always some type of non acceptance, a form of unconscious resistance to what is. The resistance is a form of judgment on the thought level. The resistance is a form of negativity on the emotional level.

Depending on how strongly you identify with your mind, the pain intensity is due to the degree of resistance in the present moment. Remember we only live in the now—the present moment—but the mind is always seeking to deny the now. The mind cannot function and stay in control without the past and present, but it perceives the present moment as threatening. Time and your mind are inseparable. Of course, we need time and our mind to function in this world. But when you allow time and mind to take over your life, that is when pain and sorrow set in.

The mind continues to cover up the present moment with the past and future. The present moment is your infinite potential of being. If you want to stop creating pain for yourself, you must truly in your heart realize the present moment is all you ever have. Always focus on living in the present moment. When you are living your life in the past and the future, which is in time instead of the now, you are creating inner resistance to something that is already is. You must surrender to what is. Always say yes to the present moment, which is life. You will see how life will suddenly start working for you rather than against you.

Here's the secret: Nothing will ever happen in the past, it happens in the now. Nothing will ever happen in the future, it will happen in the now.

What you think of as the past is a memory trace, which is stored in the mind of a former present moment. When you think of something from the past, you reactivate a memory trace. Thinking of something in the future is an imagined present moment; it is a projection of the mind. When you think of the past or present, it is only done in the present moment because we only live in the now. So obviously the past and the future have no reality of their own; their reality is only borrowed from the present moment.

When you are able to accept and appreciate the now—the present moment—the more you will become free of pain and suffering.

Therefore, *stop* living your life worrying about what you did or did not do in the past. *Stop* worrying about what you think will happen or will not happen in the future.

f

RESONATE WITH YOUR DESIRES

You must get into vibration resonating with your dreams. Remember feeling is conscious awareness of your vibration. If you are feeling sad, you are vibrating on a low frequency. Emotions are the vibrations. We have the ability to cause ourselves to vibrate however we want.

Mind and body is in vibration. It is very important to have them in a high vibration. When we do that, we do our best work.

As spiritual beings, all "the know" is in us. Spirit is 100% evenly present in all places; it is everywhere equally present all the time and at the same time. It is all knowing! It is all power!

That is right! All the know, all the power is within you! And it is your responsibility to tap into it and use it, to open up so knowledge flows to you and through you. You must be on the frequency to attract what you want.

Tap into this infinite world. Hold the mental image of your desire. If you hold the idea in your mind, by law it must move into physical form. That is perpetual transmutation of energy. You do that with your creative faculties in your intellect faculties. The more you understand, the more you use it, the more you will improve the quality of your life.

I'm going to take a brief moment to help you understand the natural law of perpetual transmutation. It explains that everything in the universe that we can see, hear, smell, taste, or touch, together with our emotions, is the manifestation of energy in various levels of vibration. The universe as a whole has its existence in an ocean of motion. And motion is the only thing that is constant. Change is energy's only attribute. Energy is in a constant state of transmission and transmutation. It is the cause and effect of itself and can be neither created nor destroyed.

6

LAW OF SUPPLY

Believe you can and you're halfway there.

–Theodore Roosevelt

LAW OF SUPPLY

There is an unlimited supply of every good you can imagine. I love how Jesus stated in the new testament, "Ask and it shall be given to you, Seek and you will find, Knock and it shall be opened to you" (Matthew 7:7). That is a powerful statement, it's real.

We are never satisfied. God did not intend for us to be forever satisfied. You should be happy and grateful with what you have, but never satisfied. The law of our being is ceaseless for increase, progress, and growth. When one good is realized, become aware that another desire for a greater good will develop. Thus, when a higher state is reached, another more fabulous state will unfold and urge you even higher. The advancing life is the true life, the life God intended for us to live.

There is a world within – a world of thought and feeling and power; of light and beauty, and although invisible, its forces are mighty.

–Charles Haanel (1866-1949)

SOURCE TO YOUR SUPPLY

God is our source. We are living in an abundant universe. There is an infinite source of supply, which is ours for the asking and giving thanks. We must see all the good that we want and know that it is flowing freely to us.

I have a motto I live by: "Ask not, receive not." Of course, I must ask, believe, and then receive. So whom do I ask? My Supreme Power, "Super" God. I connect with Him daily through loving others and gratitude. In the "natural," I ask the person in charge of that particular situation. When loving others and gratitude are combined, I get "supernatural" results. My faith is in God, not the person I am asking to help me.

Everything comes from the universe. Your desires are delivered to you through people, circumstances, and events, by the law of attraction. When I think of the law of attraction, I think of it as the law of supply. It is the law that gives power for you to draw from the infinite supply. When you release perfect frequency of what you want, guess what? The perfect people, circumstances, and events will be attracted to you and delivered!

You must remember it is not the people who are giving you the things you desire. If you think that, you are holding a false belief, and you will surely experience lack because you are looking at the outside world and people as the source to your supply. When the true supply is invisible, you may call that Infinite Intelligence, God, Supreme Mind, Universe, Energy or whatever else you want to call it. It's the same description, just different terminology. Therefore, whenever you receive anything, keep in mind that you attracted it to you, by the law of attraction, by being on the frequency and in harmony with the universal supply.

When You Desire a Certain Thing

You have the power within you to manifest your desires. You must educate your mind to a larger state of thinking. When you can think and see by faith more abundance, you will receive more abundantly.

The universe is filled with all the necessary substance for every imaginable good you can imagine. And yes! You are entitled to a full and ever-increasing supply of any and every good you may need or desire.

Jesus stated, "What things soever you desire, when you pray, believe that you receive them and you shall have them." You may ask, how do we believe that we shall have what we asked? We make an agreement;

this means you must open up to the miracle that is seeking you as much as you are seeking it. Ask your supreme power (God, Universe, Spirit, etc.) for whatever your heart desires, believe that your supreme power has given you what you asked, thank your supreme power for what you asked for, and continue to give thanks. Listen to your intuition, act, and you shall receive.

To rely on and believe in your unlimited potential and power, you must understand how faith functions. Faith is substance, hope, and evidence not seen. Faith is confident belief in the truth. Faith is the head chemist of our mind. When faith is combined with the vibration of your thoughts, the subconscious mind instantly picks up the vibration, translates it into its spiritual equivalent, and then transmits it to the infinite intelligence.

Faith is certainty; it's when you know that you know that you know!

7

LAW OF
ATTRACTION

The winners in life think constantly in terms of I can, I will, and I am. Losers, on the other hand, concentrate their waking thoughts on what they should have or would have done, or what they can't do.

–Denis Waitley

LAW OF ATTRACTION

The law of attraction states like attracts like. Whatever is transmitted into the universe is attracted to energies that are of an equal frequency, resonance, or vibration.

The law of attraction is working in your life whether you know it or not. Many people are aware of the term *law of attraction*. There are some who do not believe in it, but it's still working in their life.

The people who do not believe in the law, do not know about the law, or do not understand the law use words like these to describe it: *out of the blue, luck, meant to be, fate, karma,* and the famous word *coincidence*.

You attract that which you concentrate on. Your thoughts are powerful energy, which causes your feelings. If you are feeling positive emotions, you will attract to you positive life experiences. If you are feeling negative emotions, you will attract life experiences of negativity. Thus, if you desire love, peace, happiness, great health, abundance, serenity, and total life prosperity, you must feel what it already feels like in your life right now. Remember, we only live in the now.

Law of attraction delivers to you what you want and what you do not want, depending on the signal you send into the universe. The universe says, "Your wish is my command."

All the things you want are made of energy, which is vibrating too. Everything is made up of the exact same thing whether it's your hand, chair, ocean, or stars. Everything is energy.

We are the most powerful transmission tower in the universe. We are eternal energy. We are energy magnets; we can electrically energize everything to us and electrically energize ourselves to everything we want. We humans manage our own magnetizing energy. No one outside of you can think or feel for you. Your thoughts and feelings create your frequencies.

The hardest part about the law of attraction is knowing how to keep yourself in the mindset you must be in to attract positive results into your life. It is hard to think positively about what you want, especially when you are among negative people or bad things. It is easy to think negatively. That is why I am revealing the other essential natural universal laws throughout my book.

To become conscious of this power is to become awakened. When your mind touches the universal mind (God), it receives all its power. This truly is the great secret to life. Now you do not have an excuse for not walking in your power. Contact me *www.KaninaJohnson.com* and I will continue to guide you to your desires.

How to Get the Law of Attraction to Give You What You Desire

When you truly desire something, you set up a line of force that connects you to whatever you desire. When you live your life by walking in "love" and continual gratitude, you stay connected to the original source, God.

Get a clear image of your desire. If it is a red Ferrari convertible, clearly form the image of the red Ferrari convertible, look at a picture, or even better, see the car in person, touch it, sit inside, and, of course, take it for a spin. Ask your supreme power, thank your supreme power. Hold the mental image of it with the most positive certainty that it is on the way to you. After you form the thought, have absolute and unquestioning faith that the car is coming. You are never to think of it or speak of it without feeling confident that it will arrive. Claim it as already yours. As you are holding the image, listen to your intuition, act, and you shall receive.

You have impressed your thoughts upon thinking substance. The red Ferrari convertible will be brought to you by the power of the supreme intelligence, acting upon the mind of mankind. The thinking substance is in everything, it communicates with everything. It desires you to have more life and better living, which caused the creation of the Ferrari.

The thinking substance will do whatever people set in motion by their desire, faith, and acting in a certain way. You can have anything you want, as long as you use it for the advancement of your own life and lives of others.

God, the one substance, is trying to live, do, and enjoy things through you. The desires you feel for abundance is the infinite seeking to express Himself in you. You need not hesitate to ask largely. You are to focus and express the desires of God. Leave the how to Him. Remember you must be active; your desires will not just fall in your lap.

STEPS TO BUILD REALITIES

The three steps to create reality in your life are interest, attention, and expectation. When you follow the steps closely, you will notice where you fail to attract your desires. You do not have to worry about where you are off track with your thinking; you just need to get on track. I'm revealing these steps to help you develop a greater awareness of the law of attraction, so you will work with and in harmony with the law. I have learned these steps from such great masters as Raymond Holliwell, Bob Proctor, and Mary Morrissey.

Interest: What you are interested in. Interest is paying close attention to some object or thing. It is being definitely concerned about something or someone. Interest is tending to see in the outer world what is already existent in one's mind. Things you think of that give you joy, pleasure, wisdom, or satisfaction are interests.

To have high interest is not enough. You must inject that interest into your life daily. Ask yourself: What is it I am really interested in? What do I love? Then give that your attention, which leads to the next step.

Attention: Your attention must portray your interest and the sharper your interest, the more intense your attention will be. It is your attention that draws from the outside world. As you direct your attention to your interest, this magnetizes your power of attraction. It will then draw to you much of the same as your thoughts. When much of your interest is taken up with your full attention, you will notice that most of your petty and selfish leanings will be absorbed. This will occur by your higher interests, and you will steadily progress.

If you really want to improve anything in your life, take your interest and attention, and apply it directly into your life. Take what you are interested in doing, and then give it your conscious attention. That is exactly what brings focus. It is a must to give your desires attention. Whatever you give your attention to will grow.

Expectation: This is an active form of attention. Your expectation must be built up with your interest and attention. I am talking about attention with intensity. When you believe in the probability of success in your endeavor, you experience intense interest in your work. The interest is intensified with expectation and anticipation. Through this you will draw to you the success you are working for.

Thus, when you want to engage the law of attraction, you must understand that the law works through two phrases, *desire* and *expectation*. We amplify our understanding and our education in working with the law of attraction by our interest, attention, and expectation.

When our thoughts are firmly charged with the idea that there are no failures, we constantly expect success. We are living in this physical world, so we will incur what appear to be failures. You know something that happens that we consider a failure. The fact is that what looks like a failure at the time and seems like a failure is actually information.

That information when used properly will become part of our expected success. When we do that, our minds become strengthened and like a magnet, drawing to us through the principle upheld whatever desire is powerful at the time.

When we gain a broader understanding and harmony with the law of attraction, what we will understand is that everything that happens can be used for the greater good.

CREATING YOUR REALITY ON PURPOSE

When you choose your intention and then lock your attention, you have chosen to participate on purpose in the universe you are presently participating in. Think about which one you desire to choose. As far as I am concerned, I'm in this physical world but not of this world. I live in the universe of Heaven/Spirit, the universe of unlimited possibilities.

I have learned that we exist simultaneously in many different forms, dimensions, and times. We are choosing which reality we want to live in through our intentions and attention.

Quantum physics theory states you are the observer and the participant. When you have clearly defined intention and unwavering consistent attention, guess what you are doing. You have chosen which world you are going to participate in.

Scientists tell us that the things we are observing in our outer world are the projections of our inner world.

I know all of this may sound just a little unreal, so I am going to help you understand in a practical way.

Imagine you send out a vibration for the future that you want to earn $250,000 in the next year. If you are focusing on that, feeling it, acting on it, and then reinforcing it with your actions, the money starts to take physical form. Conversely, if you're putting out an intention of $250,000, and you stress out when your bills come in, and you keep telling your friends how broke you are and how bad the economy is, then these vibrations cancel each other out.

Whenever you think, feel, and act broke, or worry about the economy, you are sending out a vibration that is bound to cancel your intention. This is why so many people struggle with manifesting the things they desire in their lives. In other words, only vibrations that are in resonance with each other can harmonize. This is the scientific principle behind the law of attraction.

We create our reality on whichever dimension we choose to participate; it is very important that your thoughts, feelings, and emotions are in harmony with your actions. If they are not in sync, your present and future won't harmonize. They will intercept, and they will cancel each other out.

Can you see how setting your desire or intention in the present is creating your vibration and equates with how you are choosing to participate in the universe? If the vibration you are offering is out of resonance or harmony with what is coming back from your future, you won't be able to create it.

This is why making a decision based on where you are going, not where you are, is so critical. The key is to accept where you are without resistance. You accept "what is" without fighting it, but you keep your intention on your desire. This is the secret to manifestation.

If you remain at this high level of vibration, you must realize that you don't have to create your desire. It is already created, but you just have to align with it. What you desire is in the quantum field of possibilities, what some refer to as alternate universe. So get in harmony with it, start taking action based upon it, and that is what will unfold.

f

I wish this is bringing you a new awareness, a lesson or a manifestation that you are making progress; of course, that is *if you look for it*!

8

LAW OF
RECEIVING

" *For it is in giving that we receive.*

–St. Francis of Assisi "

THE LAW OF RECEIVING

The law of receiving states: In order to receive, you must first give. A lot of people have this in reverse. This is an absolute law of the universe, and all of us are subject to this great law. It works similarly to the law of cause and effect. Now, you may allow your mind to dwell on the fact that you don't have much for yourself right now. So you say to yourself, how could you possible give more to others? This is a point that many people come to, and by reading this chapter of my book, you will understand that the avenues in which you can give are infinite, and so are the avenues of receiving.

I love the scripture in the Bible that states, "Give and it shall be given unto you." Good measure running over. I interpret God the law as saying, "As you give, I will open up the windows of heaven and pour upon you such a blessing." You must give from the heart. If you are giving to get back, you are trading; this is what not to do. Just give gratefully, and it will come back.

You can give through many different avenues and in many different ways. It could be as simple as holding the door open for someone. Give a total stranger a smile to help brighten that person's day. There is no form of giving that is better or more favorable than anything else. Giving is giving. When you give a smile with an open heart, that is as impacting as writing and giving a check for $10,000. Giving is giving.

You must give more to receive more. Do not get hung up on the money subject. When you eliminate the limiting thoughts of, "I don't have enough money to do...," you will open your mind to huge possibilities. Money can play a role in giving for sure, but it is not the only means to express opulence.

Look for opportunities to give everywhere you go. I'm talking about giving to every single person you see. Just give a nice smile, hold the door, or even give a hug. You will be surprised how good it makes that person feel and how you feel. As you focus your mind on ways in which you will give, you will automatically find ways in which to serve. The more ways you find in which to serve, the more money will flow to you because money is the result of service.

Make giving a habit. The more you give, the more you receive, and the more you receive, the more you can give. Now that is a beautiful cycle!

Stay in harmony with the law of giving. Naturally, in the law of life, there is a good that cannot be contained that makes itself available and known to us. No matter how big a container we bring, it is always bigger. Look here! We are dealing with the infinite, and we have infinite potential. That's right! There is no end to your potential; you are powerful beyond measurement.

Sowing and Reaping

Sowing means planting "seeds" of service and helping the planet as well as others. There is a season in which to sow seeds, and there is a season in which to reap a harvest, but you never do both at the same time. You cannot plant seeds and harvest the next day; by natural universal law, the gestation period must elapse. The only thing you can do is to make sure you are planting seeds of service each and every day, to as many people as possible.

Reaping means collecting the fruits of your labor, and enjoying the benefits of living in harmony with the laws of success. Remember, the more you sow, the more you reap. This is an inescapable law that, unfortunately, for some works both good and bad.

You can do both in many different ways, as I stated earlier. You can serve, give, and be opulent in many different avenues. The more you look for opportunities to serve and give, the more opportunities come your way to do just that. I can assure you that you will be delighted with the results.

Sow the best service of which you are capable each and every day. You should "sow" in the best way possible by doing all acts in a truly great way. Do everything like you were doing it for God.

Sow into people's lives in your family, extended family, and even for complete strangers. You may not be related, but remember, we are all connected, we all are one, and we all have the same Heavenly Father.

Love everyone unconditionally with grace, and you will shine with joy as you move throughout your day.

Sowing and reaping are two different seasons that happen at different times; this is worth repeating. Most people plant a seed of service and expect an instant return. Well, it just does not work this way.

There is a difference between giving and trading. We really have been conditioned to trade. When we give while simultaneously expecting to receive something in return, we are not giving; we are trading. Just give what you can, where you are.

Always be sowing; remember, do not forget to sow. This is the one sure way to have a constant stream of good pouring all over you. This reminds me of the scripture that stated: "Goodness and mercy will follow you all the days of your life."

Always extend your service as much as possible. You do this by asking the most important question in business and life: How can I extend the service I render to my customers, community, and the world?

Always have new and better services to offer. This may seem very challenging, and, in fact, it is. But you can be assured of a constant inflow of new ideas by asking constant and powerful questions. The moment you stop getting ideas is the moment you stopped asking questions; it is as simple as that.

NOTHING HAPPENS BY CHANCE

This is an undeniable law that works just as accurately as the law of gravity. The human dilemma is that we have a hard time believing in things that we cannot see.

Universal laws always work even though we cannot see them, but we can see their results. Just as you cannot see the wind, you can see the results of the wind in the trees. It is the same with our results and with the laws. You cannot see the laws; you can only see their results in your life.

Gravity is a universal law. Everything in the material universe is subject to the law of gravity, including you.

What you put out will come back to you every single time, just as surely as you throw a pen in the air. It is sure to come back after you throw it in the air.

Luck is for people who let life happen to them. Luck is a term created a long time ago by someone who did not believe in divine intervention or universal laws. No, luck is not for you. The person who waits for luck to come will leave this world the same way he or she came into this world: no hair, no teeth, and no money.

Be a success by law, not by luck. Don't wait for success to come to you because it never will. Do not sit idle saying you have faith that your dream life will come to you because you must move towards your dream life. Then your dream life will move towards you.

EXCHANGE IN ABUNDANCE

Give an abundance of yourself to receive abundance. Make all your business transactions, relationships, and conversations with the intention of exchanging abundance! You see, the more abundantly you give, the more you will automatically receive in return. You will see the results of this; no matter how small, your belief will be reinforced through experience, and your expectation will skyrocket! That is how you pick up momentum, and why the rich get richer and the poor get poorer.

If you give life your best, life will give you the best. If you love life, life will love you right back. As you maintain the opulent state of being, the universe, God will surround you with the people, circumstances, and events that reflect your state of being. That is the law.

Do all tasks in a great way. Every act, no matter how small, can play a major role in the completion of your goal. It is important to complete every single act in a great way.

Constantly improve every single day; even if it is only 1% improvement, you will be amazed at the end result. Improvement of 1% every single day is 365% improvement in a year. Imagine what your income would be if you increased it by 365%.

The best way to give is to give of yourself. Remember, this is service. Give of yourself, and give others your most natural and developed talents, whenever you possibly can.

WHAT DO YOU HAVE TO GIVE?

You don't need any money to begin giving abundance. Money is only one means of opulence. Be opulent in word, deed, and action. Be opulent in attitude, enthusiasm, and vibration. Be opulent in conversations, problem solving, and goal setting. Just be yourself, be willing to give, and that is a place to start.

Money can be a good place to start, however, even if you only give away $5. Find organizations which can take your $5 and turn it into clean water for five people. This is a major impact.

Stay focused on giving and serving. As you focus your mind on giving and serving, money will pour over you in endless avalanches of abundance.

I have learned that absence of evidence is not evidence of absence. See with your inner eye of understanding, and know that when the gestation period has elapsed, you will receive your due diligence. But that is not in your control and is not your concern while giving. Just be, and just give.

The good can take a while, but it will return, and it will return pressed down, shaken together to make room for more. This is something you must experience to believe, and you will only believe through your experience.

You must find or create a great product, a great team, and a wise leader who is in integrity. When you have all three combined into one, then you have something truly unique, to give to someone else that will add value to that person's life. This is the key point!

If you are truly going to take action, I will happily help empower and guide you to take the next step in your journey.

f

9

LAW OF INCREASE

*Every moment of your life is infinitely creative
and the universe is endlessly bountiful.
Just put forth a clear enough request, and
everything your heart desires must come to you.*

–Shakti Gawain (B. 1948)

LAW OF INCREASE

There is an unlimited supply of every good thing.

I like to refer to this law as the law of praise because whatever you praise grows: giving praise before meals, giving praise for financial increase. I'm talking about anything. We may not believe in Aladdin the genie granting us our every wish, but there is an equivalent principle. It is not an object we carry around.

PRAISE THE LAW

Psalm 150 states: "Let everything that hath breath praise the [law] Lord. Praise ye the Lord."

To have faith in the law of increase, you must have a clear understanding of the law. And that understanding gives us ability to use the law, work with the law, and be in harmony with the law. We may not believe in the genie granting us our every wish, but this principle is equivalent. Putting the law to use in our life, we are stimulating our goods. In an amplified way, you will attract everything that is required for you to live a deep satisfying life that make a difference.

The understanding lies in the actual act of praise. As we give praise for our goods, we begin to move in a greater understanding through the practice. As we actually experience the feeling of gratitude and express spoken appreciation, our attraction energy get stronger, and we receive a stronger image of ourselves.

All of our thoughts act through an invisible ether. When we give praise to our richness and opulence, our thoughts increase greatly.

Praise affects our inner self to the point that our memory begins to retain all the praiseworthy thoughts we send to it.

Praise is complementary to faith. Faith is wisdom and understanding. Praise is the act of putting to special use that understanding. Faith holds a substance of power; praise is the fuel that generates that power into an active force. When you express praise, it is a stimulant of the mind. It quickens the answers to your prayers. It speedily transforms the goods you desire into a usable, visible substance.

When we give praise, we open ourselves upward to God. We then lift our consciousness to a higher realm. You become a greater channel so that you may receive the good that is waiting to come to you.

We should give praise in faith. Most of us praise after we receive, which only gets us into a rut. Anyone can easily be grateful once that person has received his or her desired good. If conditions are bad, we often forget to give praise. If you continue to give praise despite adversity, you will notice the adversity will soon disappear. This is not some fairy tale or a promise; this is universal natural law.

In the Bible, Jesus states, "What things so ever ye desire, when ye pray, believe that ye receive them and ye shall have them." Praise is what Jesus is speaking of, belief in action.

GRATITUDE

Gratitude keeps us connected to God. Many people live their life consciously rightful in many ways, but continue to live in poverty due to lack of gratitude. When we are always grateful, we live in close touch with God. The nearer we live to the source of everything, the more we will receive.

When you put effort into being grateful, God will move swiftly to give you desires of your heart. Your mind is led by gratitude along the ways by which things come.

Gratitude can keep you looking toward the infinite. There is no end to our potential. It will prevent you from focusing on lack. It is the natural principle that action and reaction are always equal and in opposite directions.

Since the grateful mind is always focused on the best, it will receive the best. You will constantly expect good things. Your expectation becomes faith. You will then have certainty; when you know that you know, then you know! As you truly absorb this, fear will vanish because you know you can have whatever your heart desires.

Remember, you cannot fully walk in your power without gratitude. It is gratitude that keeps you connected with power.

IMPRESSION OF INCREASE

Impression of increase is what every man and every woman is seeking. It is the urge of the power formless intelligence, God, within us seeking fuller expression. We are always seeking more life: desiring more food, clothes, better living, more knowledge, pleasure, beauty, and luxury.

All things are governed by increase. We are a creative center; urge of increase has been given to all of us. People instinctively know this, so they are forever seeking more. Because it is the deepest instinct of our natures, all men and women are attracted to another person who can give them more of the means of life. When you allow increase of your life to cease, apathy sets in at once.

Communication is critical to success in this modern media world in which we all live. As we deal with other people, whether directly, by e mail, by phone, or letter, our key thought must transfer to their mind the impression of increase.

You must convey the impression of advancement with everything you do. No matter how small the transaction, even if you are dealing with a small child. As you act in a certain way, people will receive the impression that you are an advancing person, a person of importance that helps all with whom you deal.

To walk in this power, you must hold the unshakable faith that you are in the way of increase. Let this faith inspire, fill, and permeate all your actions. Words will not always be necessary to communicate increase. People will feel the sense of increase when they are in your presence. They will be attracted to you.

When providing a service, you must give others a use value greater than the cash value you are taking from them. As you take honest pride in doing this, people will return where they are given increase. Here's the power! The supreme power which desires increase in everything and knows everything will move you toward people who have never heard of you. You will increase rapidly, and you will be surprised at all your unexpected blessings.

However, in receiving all of this, you must never lose sight of your vision of what you want or of your faith and purpose. You must never seek to control or have power over other people; this will weaken your power.

10

LAW OF
COMPENSATION

"*The good life is expensive. There is another way to live that doesn't cost as much, but it isn't any good.*

—Spanish Distiller

MONEY

Money is a servant! You should earn the amount of money you need to provide for the things you want and live the way you choose. Material wealth is a normal and natural state for you to live in. Always remember to love people and use money. Do not be tempted to reverse this equation regardless of the circumstances.

It is imperative you begin to see money as a diligent obedient servant you employ to earn more money. The wealth you are seeking is seeking you in return. So, open wide the doors of your conscious mind "power center," and begin to receive now!

WHAT YOU SOW YOU SHALL REAP

Jesus stated, "Whatsoever a man sow, that shall he also reap." Thus, you do not have to worry about someone beating you, about someone not being honest. When you are dealing with the infinite, the supply is unlimited. You can never take more than your share. You see, someone who is not being honest in dealing is not working with the infinite. That person's supply is limited.

Lack and limitation only exist when we allow for them in our mind. But prosperity consciousness knows no lack or no limitation. Many of us are far less aware of our own power.

When you understand the natural law of compensation, it can be the law that is the key to all the dreams you have ever had. This law helps us to understand who we really are. We are God's highest form of creation. You can lift yourself out of the place where you are, and then proceed to the place of success and plenty, where you rightfully belong. Remember, you can have anything you want! If you fail to realize that, a mistake is being made. You are having the wrong image of yourself and not relating to the law correctly. You see, the law does not change; you must change. All the success and prosperity is already here.

Your failure to meet the demands of life is not material; it is a failure within yourself, a lack of understanding. It does not matter what your problem is, the law can work it out. Of course, you must adjust your thinking to work with the law.

THE LAW OF COMPENSATION

The law of money states that the amount of money you earn will be in exact ratio to four things. This formula is as exact and unfailing as the law of gravity. It will work every time with every person.

Understanding and compliance with this law will ensure you receive large sums of money on a constant basis. Overflow!

The amount of money you and I earn is in exact ratio to these four things:

The need for what you do: Is there a definite need for the services you are rendering? If you are trying to sell records to the masses today, you will be out of luck. There is no major demand for that product. There must be a need for what you are doing.

Your ability to render your service: This is the second and most important piece of this puzzle. You must be very good at rendering the service or selling the product. The entire equation rests on this aspect. There must be a need for what you do, and you must become very good at filling that need.

f

The difficulty to replace you: The better you get, the more difficult you will be to replace. No one is more valuable as a person, but some people have chosen to develop more skills than others.

The quantity of the services/products delivered is the last phase of this equation: If you are very good at styling hair, the only limit you will have is the quantity or volume of business you can handle. The more people you serve, the more money that will flow to you. This is a difficult transition, and one very few people make.

Select something you love to do, and begin mastering it. Master it, get amazingly good at it, and people will come from all over the world to be served by you. You will be a servant to millions.

How "The Big Money" Flows to You

Napoleon Hill stated:

> When money comes in quantities known as 'the big money,' it flows to the one who accumulates it, as easily as the water flows down hill. There exists a great unseen stream of POWER, which may be compared to a river; except that one side flows in one direction, carrying all who get into that side of the stream, onward and upward to WEALTH – and the other side flows in the opposite direction, carrying all who are unfortunate enough to get into it (and not able to extricate themselves from it), downward to misery and POVERTY.

> Every man who has accumulated a great fortune has recognized the existence of this stream of life. It consists of one's THINKING PROCESS. The positive emotions of thought form the side of the stream which carries one to fortune. The negative emotions form the side which carries one down to poverty.

> This carries a thought of stupendous importance to the person who is following this with the object of accumulating a fortune.

If you are in the side of the stream of POWER which leads to poverty, this may serve as an oar, by which you may propel yourself over into the other side of the stream. It can serve you ONLY through application and use. Merely reading, and passing judgment on it, either one way or another, will in no way benefit you.

Poverty and riches often change places. Poverty may, and generally does, voluntarily take the place of riches. When riches take the place of poverty, the change is usually brought about through well-conceived and carefully executed PLANS. Poverty needs no plan. It needs no one to aid it, because it is bold and ruthless. Riches are shy and timid. They have to be attracted.

Here is a secret to making your mind a money magnet. When helping other people get what they desire, identify their problem, and give them a solution. To attract massive wealth, you must make your solution or the answer to their problem greater than your promises. Over deliver on what you promise. Guess what? You will find yourself in the top 3% of income earners in your chosen profession.

You create permanent and lasting wealth by having people repeatedly come to you with a high level of satisfaction. They will desire to give you more money for ongoing and new problems that they have. They will feel you have the most satisfying solution.

OPULENCE

I love what Thomas Troward spoke about in *Hidden Power. The Spirit of Opulence*: The opulent mode of thought consists in cultivating the feeling that we possess all sorts of riches that we can bestow upon others, which we can bestow liberally because by this very action we open the way for still greater supplies to flow in.

If we clearly realize that the creative power in ourselves is unlimited, then there is no reason for limiting the extent to which we may enjoy what we can create by means of it.

ƒ

Where we are drawing from the infinite, we need never be afraid of taking more than our share.

We must realize the danger of not having sufficient knowledge of our own riches and looking upon the external products of our creative power as being true riches instead of the creative power of spirit.

If we have a clear understanding of the power we possess, there is no need to limit ourselves in taking what we desire from the infinite storehouse. We have the right to all things that we desire.

But we must realize that the true wealth is in identifying ourselves with the spirit of opulence.

We must be opulent in our thoughts. Do not just think money. Money is only one means of opulence. Instead of just thinking money, think opulence. You will be thinking larger, generous, and liberal. You will soon realize that powerful thoughts will flow to you.

We must not become dependent on any particular form of wealth. Nor shall we insist that it come to us through a particular channel. If you choose to think that way, you will be imposing a limitation and shutting out other forms of your wealth. We must enter into the spirit of it.

The spirit is life. Life ultimately consists of circulation throughout the universe. To help you to become clearer, let me explain what circulation is. Circulation means a continual flowing around. The spirit of opulence is no exception to the others universal laws I'm speaking about throughout this book, which is law of all life.

THE THREE WAYS TO EARN MONEY

Trading time for money is the first and worst way to earn money. This is the common way people know. Almost everyone does it, and it doesn't work very well for anyone.

Trading money for money is the second way you can earn money, but in this strategy you must have a lot of money even to begin.

Leveraging your time and efforts through multiple sources of income. This is the process wealthy people use to accumulate their wealth. This is by far the best way to earn money. It is the easiest through the technology we have available to us today, through the Internet and home based industries.

The wealthy set up multiple sources of residue income. They take risks with their money; that is the second way to earn money; their money is working for them. Many of them create a product; they did the work once and then receive continual effortless money. When they physically work, they are doing what they love; they are doing what they are passionate about. They would be spending their time doing it anyway; the only different now is they are nicely compensated.

MULTIPLE SOURCES OF INCOME

Multiple sources of income, also known as "M.S.I." is an idea that you are in harmony with. It is not another job; it is not a better job; it is not even a job.

Multiple: More than one

Source: Money earning ideas, taking form and resulting in profit

Income: Earnings coming in every form.

With the technology of the great Internet, you can sell your product and/or services and earn money without your physical presence. You can also sell other people's products and services, a situation mainly known as joint venture partnership, affiliate marketing. You can earn so much money while you are sleeping, so when you awake, you can do whatever you please. Now that's a great life!

"M.S.I." is a way of adding new excitement and fun to your life daily, while you are becoming very wealthy. Once you are occupied by this idea, you will begin to attract great wealth, because it will be attracted to you.

f

Three Points to Easily Fall Into a Delusion

If you are not succeeding and are lacking of any good thing, you must look closely to the cause. You must realize where you fail in your consciousness to think rightly. Correctly applying each of these steps will help you understand how to hold your mind and thinking, giving you access to the frequency that is in harmony with the law.

First of all: Are you expecting something for nothing? Do you seek to be the one who never pays, holding back, letting someone else pay? When you expect something for nothing, you are not in harmony with the law, which means you are not experiencing your part of the goodness. To expand your understanding and experience the free flow of the goods that are in this universe, you must participate in earning, having, and giving. Always be willing to pay your way.

Second: Are you always looking for a bargain? If you are always hunting for things that are the cheapest buy, waiting for bargain days, you will always have to take bargains. Naturally cheap thoughts can only bring cheap returns. Remember, there are no bargains in life.

To be in harmony, you must appreciate that which is a good value. Hold an image of the best value you are seeking. Your image will be a guide to how you use your energy, thought, resources, action, time, and money.

We must understand the universe is lavish. The universe creates millions of seeds of the same kind. We are one with the universe.

Third: Do you hate to pay your bills? If you hate paying your bills, you do not like to let go of the money. This may take a lot of practice. I understand! As you pay your bills, think about the service you are receiving. Put yourself in harmony with how much you appreciate the service you receive.

11

LAW OF SUCCESS

If we did all the things we are capable of,
we would literally astound ourselves.

–Thomas Edison

ESSENCE OF THE LAW OF SUCCESS

The common denominator of success is in forming the habit of doing the things that failures don't like to do.
                                                    –Albert E. N. Gray

You must first understand the definition of success. Earl Nightingale stated, "Success is the progressive realization of a worthy ideal." What he is saying is: The idea is worthy of you because you are trading your life for it. It is an ideal and not just an idea.

James Allen said it well, "An ideal is an idea that you have fallen in love with." You are in perfect harmony with the idea. When you are in love with an idea, you have become intellectually involved. You are totally in tune to the image, your true perception, and you are using your will to focus on that idea. As you continue to think of the idea, you are receiving hunches and feelings. Then you remember something to help you move closer to the desired success.

Success is not from what you do. Success is how you do it. Know that as you progress toward the idea being manifested, it is only natural you are going to fail in many attempts because you do not know how to get there. You only know you will get there. Think of a failed attempt as a feedback from the universe. The universe is letting you know it is time to self correct.

It is important to understand the difference between failing at an attempt of something and being a failure. This is a very important part of success, and it is a part most people misunderstand. Just because you fail at an attempt, and you will fail at many, does not make you a failure. People are only failures when they stop trying.

So you are wishing to succeed? Remember you already possess all of the essentials within you. You must gain the right understanding of the principles and laws that success is based upon. You must apply the right method of operating all the laws until you have earned the desired success.

When you understand how to work with them, you will be empowered to become a success in every area of your life deliberately, on purpose, and by design. You will be deliberately creating the life you want.

I will briefly help you understand the natural laws of the universe, so you may consciously apply them in your life to gain success. Keep in mind, all the laws work together. It may seem like a lot to learn and understand. But believe me, it is worth your life to learn, understand, and apply in your life on purpose. Only you hold the key to your life; God has granted it to you. Hint: "use it" and walk in your power!

The law of cause and effect: Whatever you send into the universe comes back. Action and reaction are equal and opposite. Say good things to everyone; treat everyone with total respect, and it will all come back. Never worry about what you are going to get; just concentrate on what you can give.

The law of vibration and attraction: Everything vibrates; nothing rests. Conscious awareness of vibration is called feeling. Your thoughts control your paradigms and your vibration, which dictates what you attract. When you are not feeling good, become aware of what you are thinking, and then think of something pleasant.

The law of perpetual transmutation: Energy moves into physical form. The images you hold in your mind most often materialize in results in your life.

f

The law of polarity: Everything has an opposite, hot-cold, up-down, good-bad. Constantly look for the good in people and situations. When you find it, tell the person. People love compliments, and the positive idea in your mind makes you feel good. Remember good idea, good vibration.

The law of rhythm: The tide goes out; night follows day; good times and bad times. When you are on a down swing, do not feel bad. Know the swing will change, and things will get better. There are good times coming; think of them.

The law of relativity: Nothing is good or bad, big or small, until you relate it to something. Practice relating your situation to something much worse, and yours will always look good.

The law of gender: Every seed has a gestation or incubation period. Ideas are spiritual seeds and will move into form or physical results.

Your goals will manifest when the time is right. Know they will.

Everything is subject to universal law, so is success. The exact use of the law will produce results every time.

I wanted to state those laws briefly and clearly, to help you raise your level of awareness faster. Have you noticed throughout the book, that I spoke about each of those laws and the other laws governing the universe? Remember all the laws are working in your life if you know it or not. Now, you know. Go create the life of your dreams.

USE THE LAW TO BENEFIT YOURSELF

Make a decision to succeed. Bring yourself and your actions to higher standards than the masses.

God intended for every individual to succeed in life. Whoever thinks he can, "he can." It is God's purpose that we all become great. It is God's will that each individual person should not only use, but also enjoy, every good in the universe. The law of God denies us nothing; we must raise our level of consciousness to become in harmony with God's law. We can build ourselves into a greater success. Yes, every mind can develop greatness. To become great, your soul must act and must rule your mind and body.

Wealth is our birthright. The powers inherent in us are inexhaustible; we have capacity for endless development. There are no limits to our possibilities.

Ask other successful people how they became successful.

I will let you in on a powerful secret to success. Put your energy in other people. Help as many people as you can get what they want, and you will get what you want. This is the universal law of reciprocity. Of course, your actions must be from love, if you would like to achieve your desired goal.

SUCCESS IS THE PERSONAL ADVANCEMENT

Your state in life is largely determined by your mental attitude. Successful people understand they must have a constructive state of mind, with a strong positive "I can" attitude, which will lead to successful endeavors. To have consistent success, we must have a successful attitude. The ruling mental state is the difference that decides success or failure.

A person with a negative attitude who thinks he or she cannot, will not. A person with a negative attitude is out of tune with the divine order of things.

Guess what? If you think you can or if you think you can't, you are right! Success is all in the state of mind.

When a person is radiating energy of gloom, discouragement, and failure, he or she has accepted from somewhere this "I can't" attitude. If you find yourself having those emotions, begin to focus on "I can." You will find yourself naturally gravitating toward the "I can" attitude. "I can't" is life depleting, and "I can" is life giving; you get to choose.

ƒ

Here are six characteristics every successful person has:

1. Think big "your goal."

2. Believe in "yourself."

3. Share the vision.

4. Act.

5. Focus on "the most important."

6. Never give up!

We are our own self; only you can do the six things to have success in your endeavors.

ACCOMPLISH EVERYTHING YOU WANT

To have everything you desire, you must listen to your inner self and not the negativity of the world around you. I know life may seem physically directed but life is bigger. Life is spirit directed. We have the power to direct our life anyway we want it to be.

A great secret. I know you may be saying, Kanina, you continue to say, "This is the great secret." Well, let me tell you, *Walk in Your Power* is composed of the great secrets of life. To tell you the truth, these are not secrets; it's just the majority of people are lacking the knowledge.

The truth is, we have the power to create anything. I said anything! Here is the catch! You must create whatever you want from within yourself first, envision it actually happening, and, yes, you must physically apply action. Taking action is where many people stop; then they wonder why their dream didn't manifest. The same people that do not take action are the ones that blame others or say that personal development crap does not work.

Keep this thought in your mind as you go throughout your day: "I can accomplish anything I want as long as I do not doubt myself." You have to become aware of the negative people that may be surrounding you.

Stay away from these people and their destructive thinking. Here is the secret to this: Stay around constructive thinking people; they will help you achieve what you want.

Remember the universe has all the answers. When your mind is not confused, you will be able to think clearly, which will help you understand what you really want. Ask the universe, so that the universe will know exactly what you want.

Take the time to build a blueprint of your life exactly the way you want it. You can shape and manipulate the fabric of the universe. What appears to be solid is actually an illusion; the universe is pure mind.

IMAGE OF THE BETTER AND GREATER YOU

Make a mental picture of a better and greater you, and hold it in your mind. Beginning now, think of yourself, your life, and your circumstances in a superior view. As you are mentally perceiving the better and the greater, you will reach out for the better and greater either consciously or unconsciously. Your thoughts, mental actions, desires, and words will eventually become filled with the spirit of progress. Then your intellectual creative faculties will grow stronger, and your powers will increase.

When you take a superior view of yourself, that is your image power to imagine a life of what you really seek to experience, be, do, or become. Allow yourself to enter into the imagine capacity, take a superior view of all that is possible, and then begin to hold that view. Stay in the spirit of "I can," and you will be holding the key to a successful attitude.

Know in your heart you can succeed, and proceed to think, live, and act in that strong conviction. You may have been searching everywhere to discover the mystic secret of success. Well, the mystery is revealed; it is two little words, "I can." You can now embrace the "I" that can be your source, being the very essence of who you are that gives rise to life itself, as the real you.

f

When you truly think you can, you will begin easily to develop the power that can. Look here! This is no miracle. It is a demonstrable law of mind. The law works this way naturally. You want persistently to think that the authentic you can do what you want to do. And let me tell you! It will not be long before you begin to find yourself actually doing a form of that thing, or better yet, actually that thing.

Here is the secret: The principle involved, if you adopt "I can" attitude, is that your mind will proceed to direct all energies into the proper faculties. Those faculties are directed toward doing what you desire to accomplish, constantly building up until they become strong enough to actually perform what you once thought was impossible.

You will realize what you used to think were difficult great obstacles are no longer difficult to conquer. When you view obstacles from a higher point of view, you will see they are always stepping stones to success.

LAW OF SUCCESS WILL GIVE YOU COURAGE AND CONFIDENCE

Understand the law will give you courage and confidence. The law is always working. Whatever we lack, the universe has. Whatever it appears you lack, spirit has. Whatever you need, spirit can supply. Whatever obstacle you encounter, the spirit of life within you and about you can overcome it.

You must truly know in every circumstance, you are greater than the things or the condition. You are a spirit of life, and the spirit of life is greater than any condition. Whatever you aim at, you must be certain of this one thing: The power to achieve it is within you. Keep the "I can" attitude, and constantly affirm what you desire. God bless!

SUCCESS FORMULA

Consciousness, or conscious awareness, is a subject that most people give very little thought to, yet it governs our success in life. The more you raise your level of consciousness, the more you will improve the quality of your life. The higher you raise your consciousness, the more your creativity will flow.

The more creative you become the more you will attract powerful connections.

Connections are what enable you to leverage yourself, your time, and your ideas. The connections you attract accelerate the growth in creating your success. Other people contribute to your success probably more than any other single component. The more connections you attract, the greater will be your success.

ſ

12

LAW OF
FORGIVENESS

" *Holding on to anger is like grasping a hot coal with the intent of throwing it at someone else; you are the one getting burned.*

–Gautama Buddha (563-483 BC)
"

IMPORTANT OF FORGIVENESS

"Forgive and you shall be forgiven" (Luke 6:37). Grasp the concept: When someone commits an act of sin against you, their behavior is unconscious. Jesus stated, "Forgive them for they know not what they do." When you can forgive, you will always be greater than the forgiven. You are superior and greater than your adversary.

We are all governed and subject to natural laws of this universe. When one of us misuses or violates the law, we call that mistake *sin*. Actually, sin is a mistake, misunderstanding, and a misjudgment. When we disobey the law, whether it is mechanical or spiritual, it is a mistake. The only method of adjustment is by correction. The only means to alter and correct the mistake is by repentance and forgiveness. They are the only means that will stop us from suffering the painful consequences of a mistake. They will enable us to become in harmony with the law again.

To truly forgive, we must forgive the person, forsake, and forget the thought or circumstance that prompted the sin. Forgiveness is the priority requirement that allows us to be in harmony with the law of our being. Forgiveness is not something that benefits the other person. Forgiveness benefits you.

IF YOU CHOOSE NOT TO FORGIVE

If you have chosen not to forgive someone, you are only harming yourself. You have placed yourself in the wrong vibration, and then your body starts to break down, causing a period of suppressed grief and anxiety, a body of dis ease, due to a lot of sinful thoughts getting bottled up and suppressing the mind.

When we violate the law, we put ourselves in a bad vibration, and all kind of things begin to happen, causing all kinds of frustrations.

As long as we are having negative thoughts, they are thoughts of obstruction in our mind, and our abundance will not flow freely. When we choose to understand that, we will want the freedom for all because that is all you will see. When I look at someone and see lack and limitation in that person's life, I'll begin to see abundance, happiness, and fulfillment. When we all can do that, this is when we are free. I shift my perception.

When you are feeling nonforgiving, you are creating a block in your awareness. To remove the block, you must shift your perception to the presence of love. Think about something you love about the person or circumstance. Think about your goals, the good you can do for others. You have placed yourself into a great vibration.

We must remember to forgive ourselves. Guilt and resentment are two of the most dangerous and damaging emotions. If you have committed a sin in the past, just release, and let it go. Really think about what kind of negative concept you are allowing to rent space in your mind. You were only functioning at the level of your consciousness at that time. As you let go and forgive, you are putting nice beautiful energy in your mind. You then will be thinking great thoughts and moving in the right direction.

Remember, any place in your life you are not at ease, know that you have thought wrongly. But of course, you can choose again. Thoughts of discord and disagreements are all around. The moment you are aware, knock it off, and focus on good thoughts.

Keep this in mind of what not to do. Conflict and argument mean you allowed someone else to take control of you. A problem cannot be solved at the same level of awareness it occurred.

13

LAW OF SACRIFICE

" *The important thing is this:*
to be able, at any moment, to sacrifice
what we are for what we could become.

–Maharishi Mahesh Yogi quotes "

LAW OF SACRIFICE

First off, a lot of us need to replace the old way of thinking about sacrifice. Many of us have grown to understand sacrifice as losing something.

Law of sacrifice is giving up something of a lower nature to receive something of a higher nature. Something always has to be sacrificed for something else. That indicates growth.

You have to give up something and replace it with something new. You must discipline yourself to do the new thing that is replacing the old.

What you are really doing is forming new habits. In order to form a new habit, old paradigms must be changed. Other people may have been responsible for making who you are, but it is your responsibility to change. Yes, it will cause a respectable amount of discomfort, but stay strong because that's where the sacrifice comes in. You give up a little discomfort, and your win will be enormous.

SOMETHING ALWAYS HAS TO BE PAID FOR SOMETHING ELSE

Everything in life has its own price. We must purchase it at the price that it demands. Each day we are saying to life and others, I will give you this if you give me that. This is sacrificing. We sacrifice each day of our life whether we know it or not. Whatever we want in life, we have to give up something in order to get it; we are sacrificing our life whether we want to or not. I see sacrifice as gaining something. If you are conscious of your transactions, you will realize you mainly sacrifice something for what you want.

You see, sacrifice is not what we have heard through our different religions. It is a definite law we all must obey. It is incapable of being avoided. No matter what we want, we have to give up something in order to get it. I truly believe many of us have been programmed to associate sacrifice with giving up, having less, and losing something. Actually, the truth is the exact opposite.

FREEDOM IS BEING ABLE TO CONTROL YOUR LIFE AND MAKING IT WHAT YOU WANT IT TO BE

Sit down and relax, decide what you really want, then take a look at what you have now.

If you desire something of great value, you must understand discipline is what leads to everything that makes life worth living. Discipline, as I see it, is giving ourselves a command and then following it. Material wealth, happiness, and peace of mind all are a result of higher levels of awareness.

To gain a true understanding of maintaining discipline, we must discipline ourselves to the study of being disciplined and gain an understanding of how our mind works. I would like for you to grasp the ideas, as you read through *Walk in Your Power*. You're reading how to live in harmony with the laws governing the universe and the power of your mind. We're all working with one infinite power.

When you live in harmony with the natural laws, you have taken control over your life. You are learning to control your thinking, not letting the outside world take charge of your life any longer. Just because you may understand the law and live your life in harmony with the law, you still must continually be learning. Only a small percentage of people live their life this way, in harmony with the law. That is why a very small percentage of people earn the majority of the wealth.

f

What do you really want? Think big! First, you must surrender your lower vibration. You must match the higher frequency that is in harmony with what you say you want. As you begin to resonate with the frequency of what you say and visualize what you really want in life, life is generous, a giver to anyone of us who place "I am," our God given name, in harmony with the frequency of what we say we want.

Here is my favorite "I am" statement. "I am" so happy and grateful now that money comes to me in increasing quantities through multiple sources on a continual basis.

WHAT DO YOU WANT?

What are your dreams; what are the things that bring you tears of inspiration? Your answers are trigger points into discovering what you truly want from your life. Stretch your mind, and imagine how you truly want to live. Do you know your life is a movie, and you are the director of your own life movies? Most people are playing extras in their own life. They could really be declaring who are the main characters, who are the extras, who comes, who goes, and what happens. You really can control your results to an enormous extent. But nothing can become real to you unless you are aware that it is real. You may have been letting life happen to you, and now you can take back your ultimate power—the power to choose.

Everyone starts with one step, and the first step is usually the hardest for most people. You will not know exactly how you will reach your ultimate goal: The *how* is none of your business; God knows how; you know *what*, and it is your job to take action in the direction of the dream.

THREE POWERFUL QUESTIONS

Who am I, what do I want, what is my purpose? If you focus on finding those answers for yourself, you will live a wonderful life on this planet. Only you know those answers, and only you can find them. No one else can tell you what your purpose is; only love can. Find your love, and you will find your treasure.

Ask yourself who you are, in order to learn about yourself more intimately. You were meant to be your own best friend, but, unfortunately, through conditioning, we are taught to beat ourselves up on a regular basis. This is not how we were meant to treat ourselves. You are the most important person in your life. If you are not operating on a high level, you cannot give anyone else your best.

Learning about yourself is extremely important because everything in your life starts with you. Remember, you are the director of your life movie. No one will give you anything; you must go out and create it.

As I have stated earlier, you must ask yourself what you really want to do with your life. I would recommend you ask this to yourself on a daily basis. You will never run out of answers if you keep asking questions. The more you ask, the better you understand; the better you understand, the more efficiently you do; the more efficiently you do, the more you will have. Work on the being, and the rest will take care of itself.

To find what you want in life, you must know what it is you are looking for. If you don't know what you are looking for, how will you know when you have found it? Most people run through life as fast as they can, looking for "something." They really don't even know that, but they know whatever it is, they don't have it, and they must get it. Only when it is too late do they realize what they were looking for was all around them.

You have talents, skills, and passions that no man or woman has ever taught you. Your purpose is unique to you, and only you can fulfill it. Do you ever wonder why you are just naturally good at different things? These are all clues into your life purpose; follow the synchronicity.

Only you can fulfill your purpose, and your purpose is not something you "have to do." Many people think it is their "slot" to live a life they don't like. They think their place in life has been set up for them, and they need to suffer through it. This is not the case. Your purpose will be the most beautiful thing in your eyes. It will bring out more passion and energy than you ever thought you could experience. It is just for you—your own unique "present" delivered from the universe, right to *you*. That is powerful!

Your purpose is your why; it is your reason for being. Without a purpose, people literally slowly disintegrate to death.

Remember this, there is no more potential in a person living in poverty than a person living in opulence. Both have the same potential; both have the same gifts: One has simply opened them up and is "playing" with them.

If you want to improve your life, I want to help you!

14

LAW OF
OBEDIENCE

" *We are not human beings on a spiritual journey.*
We are spiritual beings on a human journey.

–Stephen Covey "

LAW OF OBEDIENCE

Obey means to submit to rule or to comply with orders or instructions. Obedience governs all movement, whether mechanical, literal, or spiritual.

We live on a planet where everything operates in a very exact way. If you have not done a great amount of studying the laws that govern the universe, you will not understand law. I have noticed when people gain an understanding of the law, they have tremendous respect for it. They begin naturally to become obedient to it because they know they must obey the law. This is their reality, if they are really going to make big things happen and grow in their life.

We have been given all the materials that are required to construct the kind of life we desire. According to our obedience of the divine law and the way we use it in our daily lives, we will build in wisdom or in ignorance.

Many people assume, when they become aware that the science of living is governed by exacting laws, that living rightfully is hard. It is actually the opposite!

If we fail to obey the direction of spirit, the law of God, we will reverse good and create evil. We are 100 percent dependent on obedience for success or failure in our life.

If you choose to obey the law of fear instead of the law of God, you will have many burdens. Only as we are able to cast our burdens upon the law shall we be free. You then will live in the present, do your highest duty every day, forget your past, and let the future take care of itself.

Being disobedient to the law means you are refusing to do what you know is right.

USE THE LAW FOR YOUR BENEFIT

It is imperative to understand that the supreme intelligence is law. Once this divine knowledge of God as law is understood, you can use the law to benefit yourself. You must understand: You hold the secret of eternal happiness, peace, and dominion over all the forces around you.

We see the answer in nature. Nature is governed by the law of harmony and order. It has no burden it cannot bear. Nature knows no failures. It never plans anything but success. All of the processes of nature are successful.

Everyone who obeys the law and truly is a servant of good will become a greater soul. You will reap the power to control your every condition and enjoy an abundance of blessings.

Our problems have been due to the fact that we obey the laws of the earth more than the laws of spirit. We subject our ideas to outward appearances instead of to the inner truths. We must obey God rather than man.

It may be strange to you, but we do not own an earthly thing. It all has been loaned to us according to our understanding of the law we serve. We were born naked, and we die naked. All our earthly things are stripped from us at our earthly death. Thus, our real task in life is to find our place according to our understanding. That understanding determines the way we live our life.

Obey Spirit Within Us

When we obey the spirit within us rather than the conditions around us, the law requires us first to think things into the existence from within, before we see them on the outside. Remember, thinking is the highest function that we are capable of. And everything begins with a thought.

We either serve principle or things in all that we do and think. Things are the results or events of invisible causes. Principle is the true cause and is spirit. Principle is that which we think in our minds, and things are the results of our thoughts.

When we speak of someone who is highly regarded, we are speaking of a person of principle, someone who is governed by the law of right thinking and living. A person who is not easily swayed. Someone whom you may trust absolutely, to be true to his convictions regardless of the temptations to change. No one will deny that you are a person of utmost confidence and may become the strength and leadership many are looking for, whereas the person who is easily persuaded and yields to pressure is not the person upon whom you can depend.

God's kingdom is truly all about us: awaiting our acknowledgment and obedience to His law. You must be able to interact and live with God, the law in your life, daily. You shall then live with love, joy, hope, wealth, and peace here and everywhere. Remember, it is your choice. It is ours for the decision.

The Bible states, "If they obey and serve Him, they shall spend their days in prosperity and their years in pleasure." I must say, this is totally true to me.

15

PURPOSE

" *The two most important days of your life are the day you were born and the day you discover why you were born.*

–Les Brown "

PURPOSE

To me, purpose means knowing what brings you the most love in your life—doing what you love the most in every area of your life.

To live with purpose require three things:

1. You must have a spiritual practice, so you can get quiet and still and hear the deeper wisdom beneath the ego, "edging God out";

2. To know what is unique and special about you;

3. To be of service with your gifts.

Your purpose is your why. You must know why you are doing what it is that you are doing. When you know *why*, the *what* doesn't matter. Your why helps you become persistent; it gives you strength and calms you during storms of your life. There will be times when you may question your actions and days when you are filled with doubt. It is those times when you will clearly understand the importance of having a strong and clear purpose.

If you have no defined purpose, you will have no true and lasting happiness. Your values and purpose are the sources of happiness in your life.

Becoming aware of your purpose helps you connect with the higher side of your life, the true side of you, where your creativity lies. When you know your purpose, loneliness and separation fade away. You will not be truly happy unless you are living with purpose.

For a Period of My Life, I Felt as Though I Was Living Outside of My Purpose

I had constant struggles, although I didn't think of the experiences as struggles because I knew there was a better way; I knew I wanted the best that life had to offer.

I started to search for spiritual answers. I had an intense desire to figure out why I was on earth. And who is God? After I continued to search, I began to realize God is "spirit," God is "love." Spirit is evenly present in all places at the same time. I began to realize that I'm a spiritual being, here on earth going through a physical experience, that I have been given a specific purpose for my life, and only I could discover my purpose.

I constantly read personal development books, got personal help from life and success coaches and mentors, attended seminars, and enrolled in courses to help me understand myself better.

Once I Connected to My True Purpose

My discovery was to empower people to love and accept themselves by being who they really are, creating their dreams and living a life they love. Once I discovered my life purpose, I realized I had been an unconscious competent.

As my level of life awareness rose, I started to realize I was attracting people that had the answers I was searching for and opportunities that were in line with my purpose. Not only did I recognize great opportunities; I acted on the opportunities.

What It Is Like Living Out of Harmony With One's Purpose

To live outside of one's purpose is as if everything else is wrong. It's like working with a broken compass; you think you are going north, but you are going south. You are not sure which direction you are heading; you are just wandering.

Your purpose will be the compass that keeps you on the chosen path toward creating.

Without your purpose identified firmly in your mind, you will wander through life, never quite feeling that you are "in the flow." That's why it is imperative that you recognize what it is you are good at, what it is you really love to do. Your purpose in this lifetime is to do the thing that you love.

WHAT TO DO AS AN INDIVIDUAL WHO NOW KNOWS YOU ARE LIVING OUTSIDE OF YOUR PURPOSE

The first step you must take is becoming aware of what things, people, or events inspire you and bring you inspiration. Your inspiration will lead you to your purpose and the life you want.

Ask yourself these questions to help you begin the process of discovering your purpose:

1. What in my present day to day activities do I love doing?
2. What has meaning and heart for me?
3. What subjects am I passionate about?
4. What do I feel inspired or compelled to change in the world?

You may find you have to continue to ask yourself these questions. Once you have figured out what you are passionate about, ask your family and friends:

1. What am I doing when I'm at my best?
2. What do you consider me to be world class at?

Be willing to examine who you are!

Most people are wondering why their life is not going the way they want it. Well, they are focusing on what they do not want. They become deeply involved in their circumstances, so that they do not see all the signs the universe is giving them.

HOW YOUR PURPOSE CAN ACTUALLY HELP YOU MAKE DECISIONS

Your purpose can help you make decisions that are in line with your purpose. We sometimes forget the amount of impact a single decision have on our life and the lives of others.

Your purpose is your filter that helps you overcome what appears to be a failure. It keeps you moving. Everyone has failed at some point in his or her life. You cannot have success without failure, and you cannot have failure without success. Failure is essential to living a truly successful life. We have been conditioned to believe that it is a bad thing, but it is not. Failure is essential because that is when you will learn the most.

I have noticed many times what appeared to be a failure in my life. Well, the actions I had taken were actually leading me to my purpose.

There are only three questions you need to answer when deciding, and these questions will serve as filters through which you will make your decisions. Ask yourself these three questions, and you will be able to make decisions quickly, accurately, and with commitment.

1. Is it in harmony with my purpose? This is the first question and the most important. You should really think about this: if what you want to do is in harmony with your life purpose. If the answer is no, you do not take action. If the answer is yes, you move to the next question.

2. Will this move me in the direction of my dream? Will taking this action move you closer toward your dream or take you farther away? You must structure all of your actions in such a way that most everything you do is moving you closer to your dream. If the answer is no, throw it out. If the answer is yes, you must move to the next question.

3. Does this violate the rights of others? Is this in harmony with laws of the universe or God? Will taking this action benefit all parties? If the answer is no, you do not move forward. If the answer is yes, take the action now!

ƒ

UNDERSTANDING WHO YOU REALLY ARE

I believe that you are well aware of the day you were born. If you have not done so already, take the time to discover why you were born. Make "today" the day you discover why you were born! It really does not matter how much time it takes. You see, all that matters is that you devote the amount of time it takes until you discover your purpose. I suggest you stop now and state your purpose in as few words as possible. It's time to sit down and have a serious truth session with yourself. It's time to listen to your inner voice and give serious attention to what comes naturally to you.

You are not on this planet to live someone else's dream. So, what is it you love to do? And do not worry about what anyone else says. What's most important is that, when you truly believe you have found your purpose, do not allow yourself to be persuaded by others' opinions.

The key to your life is to do what you really love. Fall in love with an idea. That is your life! That is your purpose! Your purpose will be the compass that keeps you on the chosen path toward your ideal life.

This is your moment. This is your time to make things happen for you in a way that you never thought possible.

When you have the right purpose, you will easily develop the right vision.

VISION

Dream lofty dreams, and as you dream, so shall you become. Your vision is the promise of what you shall one day be. Your ideal is the prophecy of what you shall at last unveil.

–James Allen

WHAT IT REALLY MEANS TO HAVE A CLEAR VISION

Your vision is a clear mental picture of future results you want to experience in every area of your life. Having a vision for your life inspires and guides you every day in all your actions. It gives your life meaning and purpose.

You could say the vision represents *what* you are doing with your life, and purpose is *why*. You must know what you are going to do, and you must know why you are going to do it. To be clear, the *why* will come before the what every single time. Don't think about *what* you will be doing until you have clarity regarding *why* you want to do it.

It is your map to fulfilling your purpose. It is how your purpose takes physical form. It is your hope for a bigger and better future. The vision you hold determines the frequency of your thoughts. The larger and clearer the vision, the more bigger and better effective ideas will flow into your consciousness.

This is your ultimate reality. Imagine living the life of your dreams, and it will be much like hovering over your house in a helicopter and watching yourself living the way you really want to live. See yourself in every detail. Feel how that will feel, and you will be amazed at how your vision will come to life in your mind. And then in your life.

LIFE WITHOUT A VISION

Living a life without a vision can be depressing; you're going to feel bad about yourself and what you're doing. It feels as though you are going in circles. If you do not have a vision of who you want to be, how you want to succeed, or what you want out of life, you begin to lack drive, and your life becomes just an order of events.

Without a purpose and vision, you will always be looking outside yourself for answers. This is a clear indication that you're not with purpose. When you have the right purpose, you'll easily develop the right vision.

f

The First Step to Take to Build Your Vision

The first step you must take to build you vision is to start by asking yourself powerful questions. Powerful questions create powerful answers. The biggest and most complicated questions have answers.

Know exactly what you want. If you have a hard time creating a vision, ask yourself where you want to see yourself in so many years. Do you want to be healthy? Wealthy? Tell yourself specifically how you picture your life. Anything is possible within a vision, when you build your vision big.

When you create a successful vision, you begin to feel passionate about it. The only way to be successful in your vision is to visualize it and set goals and a plan of action to reach it. Over time, you will begin to see more parts of your vision coming true, until one day you see yourself living your vision.

A vision is the capability to see beyond your current reality, creating and inventing what does not yet exist and becoming what you are not right now. A vision is important in all aspects of life. Building your vision does not have to be difficult, as long as you know exactly what it is you see for yourself in the future.

Important things to remember when creating a vision:

1. Know exactly who you are.

2. Brainstorm, imagine, and dream.

3. Focus on things that give your life purpose and meaning.

4. Do not put limits on your dreams.

The most important aspect to this is the order that a vision establishes in your mind. The vision you are holding and impressing upon your subconscious mind, "the emotional mind," will determine what you are in harmony with. Whatever you are in harmony with you will attract.

How You Will Change When You Establish and Hold a Vision

Holding a vision, you will begin to notice changes in your emotional state. You will become aware of ideas, people, and circumstances that will help you manifest your vision.

How You Can Make Sure Your Vision Is on the Screen of Your Mind More than Your Worries

Take a long range view of all the things you want to accomplish in the future. The only criterion is that these things will help you execute your purpose. When you have it in your mind, realize that you are imaging your vision. Capture the picture, and paint it in words in a clear, concise statement.

To hold your vision, start your day reading your vision statement. As you are moving through your day, visualize your vision. Just before you go to bed, read your vision statement out loud.

When you have the right vision, you will quickly recognize the right goal.

Goals

Unless you try to do something beyond what you have already mastered, you will never grow.

–Ronald E. Osburn

Goals Is a Common Word, But So Few People Actually Have Them

I think the reason people do not have goals, is because of a lack of proper knowledge and low awareness. This is an interesting point to discuss. We do not operate in a default mode, where things just show up in our life. If we want something, to achieve something, or acquire something, we must have a plan, a strategy, and know where we are presently and where we want to *be, do, have,* or *achieve.*

If you want to have more, you must do more, and if you're going to do more, you have to be more. This is how people improve the quality of their lives.

A lot of people set a goal but never achieve their goal because they give up, either due to lack of persistence or not knowing how to reach their goal.

If we are in the habit of not setting goals, we are not being effective in our desired results. If you want to be extremely successful in business, very happy in your life, or achieve some large goal, then being effective is consistently doing the things that will bring about the results you desire.

What Is a Goal and Its Purpose?

Goals are short term steps that will lead to your vision. Your goals are stepping stones and sequential levels of life that will help you plot your course and let you know you are on the right track.

A goal gives your life direction and urgency. It's life to your purpose, keeping it crystal clear.

Goals give you focus and clarity as to what you must be doing today.

It is easy to get caught up in a big vision, without having any action patterns today. You will have a successful life if you have successful days. Successful days lead to successful weeks, which lead to successful months, which lead to successful years and so forth, until you realize you have lived a successful life.

Goals give your potential direction to work toward and will play a big role in the shaping of your daily habits. Zig Ziglar said vision tells you where you are going, habits get you there. A vision with no goals is nothing but a vision that you will enjoy mentally contemplating in your leisure hours, without ever enjoying it in the physical world.

Goal setting is a powerful process for thinking about your ideal future and for motivating yourself to turn your vision of the future into reality.

The process of setting goals helps you choose where you want to go in life. By knowing exactly what you want to achieve, you will know where you have to concentrate your efforts.

The purpose of a goal is to provide you with the necessary excitement and incentive to grow in awareness. You are a perfect expression of an infinite power. As you become more consciously aware of your oneness with the infinite power within you and its laws of expression, awareness will be reflected in your results.

Awareness gives meaning to life. The awareness you are seeking requires you to replace old conditioning. These ideas are holding you back and slowing your growth. They must be replaced with positive habits. The goal gives you a reason to do this. Goals are essential, if you want to improve the quality of your life.

AREAS OF LIFE WHERE WE SHOULD HAVE GOALS

Start with only the areas of your life where you want fulfillment.

Here are eight goal categories:

1. Career: What level do you want to reach in your career?

2. Education: Is there any knowledge you want to acquire in particular? What information and skills will you need to achieve other goals?

3. Family: Do you want to be married? Do you want to be a parent?

4. Financial: How much do you want to earn?

5. Community: Do you want to make your community a better place? If so, how?

6. Physical: Do you want good health? What steps are you going to take to achieve this?

7. Social

8. Spiritual

Evaluate your priorities for your goals:

1. Do a current personal assessment.

2. Establish and focus on those priorities.

3. Seek reasonable balance.

4. Lock in on a strategy.

5. Take action.

You already have in substance, if not in physical form, all that is necessary for you to produce any result you want in your life.

Goals must be specific. Achieving goals is a creative process. Make a clear, concise written description of your goal to crystallize the image in your conscious mind. Picture your goal in the *present*. The moment you consciously see yourself in possession of your goal, you actually have your goal on a conscious level. You want to begin thinking and talking like the person who already has the goal.

This is critical: Make sure your goals are specific and in writing, with a time frame.

Here are five good things about goals:

1. Guide and direct our behavior

2. Focus (help us to gain clarity)

3. Anticipation (give us hope)

4. Organization (cause us to organize and focus; that is when we make good things happen)

5. Progress (as long as we progress, we are moving ahead)

A Good Formula You Can Use to Have a Good List of Goals

Your first step is to make a list and prioritize the list. Decide which goal is most important to you right now. The goal should be attainable, short term, and have a realistic timeline.

1. **Make sure it's your goal,** that it's what you want for yourself because sometimes we are doing things for other people and not knowing we are doing it for others. It's our life, our most valuable asset. Sometimes we are just trying to make others happy although it's hurting us. For example, you want to be a nurse because your mom is a nurse. You must honor yourself first, and do what you want to do.

2. **Don't call it a goal.** Instead you may want to think of your goal as a promise to yourself.

3. **Clearly identify your goal.** For example, if you want to be rich, know how much money would be considered rich to you.

4. **Use the tools around you** like a life coach to help you when you bump into something that appears negative.

5. **Create a goal plan:** "What, When, Why, Who"; that's your plan. The *how* you won't know; it's impossible now to know all the steps. Just know *who* you need to help you do *what* you want to do and *why* you want to do it. Then *start!*

6. **Review plan of "when, why, and who will help you"** and keep your promise on a regular basic. As you review consciously, you will think about your goal and then new ideas will come to you.

7. **Tell yourself you will succeed** because if you tell yourself that you will succeed, you will!

8. **Tell others about your goal.**

9. **Vision your results.**

10. **START!**

A FORMULA TO TELL THAT THE PARAMETERS OF A GOAL ARE CORRECT

Timely plan your goals in three categories:

1. **Short term**: six months or less

2. **Intermediate term**: six months to two years

3. **Long term**: more than two years

Measurable: Set a precise goal, putting in dates, times, and amounts, so that you can measure achievement. If you do this, you will know exactly when you have achieved the goal, and can take complete satisfaction from having achieved it. You should take care to set goals for which you have as much control as possible. The goal should be attainable. For example, don't set a goal to be a millionaire within 30 days. There is nothing more dispiriting than failing to achieve a personal goal for reasons beyond your control.

Realistic: There is no unrealistic goal, only unrealistic time frames. We can achieve whatever we truly want, given a reasonable time frame. Many people make their goal general. The more specific, the better and easier to internalize the details.

Six keys to success:

1. Think big.

2. Believe in yourself.

3. Share the vision.

4. Execute (carry out).

5. Focus.

6. Never give up!

THINGS YOU MUST KNOW TO SUCCEED

People with goals succeed because they know where they are going.

You want to think about your goal in a cheerful, relaxed, and positive way each morning, before starting your day. Immediately it gives you something to get out of bed for. It's really giving you something to live for.

Write down your goal on a small card. Carry it with you, so you can look at it throughout the day and before you go to bed at night.

Throughout the day, when a negative thought enter your consciousness, replace it with a mental picture of your positive and worthwhile goal.

Do not be concerned with *how* you are going to achieve your goal. Rely on your supreme power, a greater power than yourself.

All you have to know is *where* you are going. The answers will come to you at the right time. Take the first step; that is all you need to know. I should write about this in every single chapter, so it will sink into all our minds because this is what holds most people back. *You will not see the second step until you have taken the first.* Why would you need to know what the second step is, if you haven't even taken the first step? Naturally, there is demand and supply. Where there is no demand, there will be no supply. You demand the second step by taking the first step.

I have a motto I live by: Ask, believe, and I shall receive. Remember, *ask*, and it shall be given to you; *seek*, and you shall find; *knock*, and it shall be open to you.

All you need is *purpose* and *faith*! Persistence is another word for faith.

The key to success is that we become what we think about. If you are thinking about your goal throughout the day, applying proper action, your goal must materialize.

Always keep in mind that the purpose of a goal is to grow, not to acquire, but to grow.

ʄ

ENLIGHTENMENT

Enlightenment is your natural state of feeling oneness with being!

Being is your essence, the feeling of your own presence. Although it is impossible to form a mental image of it, being is the true you.

Being enlightens. You will be in a state of connectedness with something that's immeasurable and indestructible. It's essentially you being one with God. It is a state of wholeness of being at one; therefore, you will be at peace. When you are enlightened, you have found your true nature beyond name and form.

When you become enlightened, you have placed a stop to suffering.

When you have not been enlightened, you will feel a separation from yourself and the world around you. That's why fear arises; you have conflicts within yourself and with the world around you. Consciously or unconsciously, you will perceive yourself as isolated; it will become the norm for you. That's why you should desire to be enlightened and bring an end to suffering, an end to continuous conflict within yourself and the world around you.

Enlightenment is rising above the level of an animal to operating in your unlimited potential. Your power! Being the true you!

Animalistic is the lowest level of consciousness just above the thinking of an animal. At this level, a person ignores the gift of life and just totally reacts to situations, barely surviving.

Mass consciousness is the level of consciousness where the majority of society stays hidden within the herd of other people, also known as *the masses*.

Although people may think at this level they are under the control of their environment, outside influences are manipulating their thinking; a person is actually unconsciously letting others think for him or her.

Although you are thinking, other people and your environment—external influences—have a big say so to how you are thinking.

At this level of awareness, people are more concerned with what others think than what they think themselves.

Aspiration: At this level, a person begins to realize there is more to life, that you can be, do, and Have more. You start to realize you no longer want to be like the mass society.

This person will still act like the mass of society but will try to think as an individual.

Individual: At this level, people begin to realize that they are unique, that no other person is like them. They begin to allow their spirit to express through them in thoughts and actions.

With clarity, integrity, and distinction, you know what you want. With this new awareness of ability, you are true to yourself; you start to notice your potential that has been inside of you all along. You start to notice what your desires manifest in your physical reality.

Discipline: At this level, people begin to give themselves a demand and follow through on the command in the time frame they set for themselves.

Living your life at this level, you are being an individual, so that you may progress to achieve your dreams that you as an individual want.

Experience: At this level a person has lived life for a long period of time at the individual and discipline levels. You are truly enlightened!

Mastery: At this level, a person is able to create and control his or her own environment by an ability to respond proactively to a situation instead of reacting without thinking.

Thinking this way you will have total peace and fulfillment in spite of circumstances.

You know who you are! You know you are a spiritual being! You know you are unique! You know you are an instrument for God, the spirit of love, to live through! You know you are in this physical world to create whatever you desire. You create!

Thinking this way provides you with the master level of thinking. You are truly letting God, the infinite intelligence, live through you. This is how you much think to walk in your God given power with purpose.

16

LAW OF LOVE

"*Love is the greatest power on earth.
It conquers all things.*
−Peace Pilgrim (1908-1981)"

Your Power

Love is an element which though physically unseen is as real as air or water. It is an acting, living moving force. It moves in waves and currents like those of the ocean.

—Prentice Mulford

Life is very simple. We have negative and positive. You get to choose! No matter, whether it is your health, work, relationship, money, or happiness, it is either positive or negative. You have great health, or you lack health. Your work is exciting or dissatisfying to you. You are engaged in happy or difficult relationships. You have plenty, or you lack money. You're filled with happiness, or you are not feeling well a lot of time.

You have the power over your entire life, and that power is inside you. Everything you desire to be, do, or have comes from love. There is no limit on love. You are made of love. The positive force of love will inspire you to move and give you whatever your heart desires.

You deserve a life of Love! No doubt! It is the power to have all the positive things you desire in life.

If I have to sum up *Walk in Your Power*, I would say it is love, the greatest power in the universe. When you live your life by the law of love, you are truly walking in your God given power. Whatever you desire is yours for the asking.

}

I may blow some of your minds! I'm not talking about the kind of love for your family or friends, because love is not just a feeling. Love is the only positive force of life!

The force of love is invisible, although we can see it everywhere in the world. Without love there is no life.

If you never thought about this, sit back and relax! Without the love of something, we would be without. If no one has the love to be an architect, we would not have a home, builder, teachers, etc. Without love, we would not have medicine, doctors, books, paintings, music. They are all created from love. Look around you right now! Enjoy the human creations that would not be in our presence without love.

So you say: Since love is my power and it is inside me, why am I not having an amazing life? Because you have a choice to harness the positive force or not. You are making the choice everyday about your life if you know it or not. I want you to know whenever you experience something not good, you didn't love, and your result was negativity. Know that love is cause of all good in your life, and the lack of love is the cause of all the negativity, pain, and suffering.

Fall in love with life! You will have no resistance; every limitation will disappear. Whatever you love will appear in your life. Your presence will be felt, opportunities will pour into your life, and your slightest touch will dissolve negativity. You will become unlimited and invincible! Are you feeling me! Now that's power!

Love is the fulfilling of the law.
—Saint Paul (Romans 13:10)

So you say: How do I fall in love with life? Well, the same way you will fall in love with another person. Think about this! You adore everything about that person! When you think of that person, you see what you love, you hear what you love, and you speak about what you love. You fall in

f

love with someone by seeing only love, hearing only love, speaking only love, and feeling love with all your heart. That's exactly how you use the power of love to fall in love with life.

Love must be the ruling force in your life. Nothing can ever be put above love.

LOVE IS LAW

The entire law is summed up in a single command;
love your neighbor as yourself.

–Saint Paul

Love is the most powerful natural law of the universe. To change your life with love, you must understand its law, the law of attraction. Attraction is the powerful force that draws people to other people. It is the attraction that draws you to your favorite things and places. The force of attraction holds together the cells of your body. It holds together every star in the universe and forms every atoms and molecule. The powerful force of attraction holds together gravity and every person, animal, plant, and mineral on earth. Check this out! It draws people to form cities, nations, clubs and groups where they are sharing common interest.

The force of attraction is the force of love. That's right. Attraction is love! When you feel attraction to your favorite food or whatever you love, you are feeling love; without love you would not feel anything. So it is right on point to say the law of attraction and law of love are the same.

The law of attraction being the law of love is the all powerful law that is keeping everything in harmony, from countless galaxies to atoms. It is operating in everything, and that means it is operating in your life. Whatever you give out, you will receive back. By natural law, whatever you give out you will attract back to yourself. Be aware what you give out in your life must return to you. Remember, you are giving out positivity or negativity through your thoughts and feelings.

It is this simple! When your thoughts are positive, they are thoughts of what you want and love. When your thoughts are negative, they are thoughts of what you do not want.

Think about this! Whatever you desire to have in life is because you love it. Would you want it if you didn't love it? I don't know about you, but I do not want what I do not love.

Most people think and talk about what they do not love, not realizing they are depriving themselves of all the good things in life. People that have a great life think and speak often of what they love. By doing this, they gain unlimited access to all the good in life. It is impossible to have a great life without love.

Nothing is impossible for the force of love. Give love and speak about what you love, and love will set you free. No matter who you are or what situation you are facing.

Love is the cause of everything positive and good in life. The positive force can create any good thing, increase the good, and change anything negative in your life.

The law of attraction, which is the law of love, is the great secret to life, the law that is operating in our life. Love is the greatest power in the universe; that is the perfect reason to love. This is your power! Since you have unlimited ability to think and talk about what you love, you have unlimited ability to bring everything good in life to you.

Giving love is the law that applies to everything in your life. The most enlightened beings throughout history told us to love others. They were not telling us to love others just to be a nice person. We were being given the secret to life! We were being given the law of attraction. When you love others, you will have an amazing life. When you love others, you will receive the life you deserve.

f

FEELING OF LOVE

> *Through your ability to think and feel,*
> *you have dominion over all creation.*
>
> –Neville Goddard

How you are feeling in any one moment is more important than anything else. Because how you are feeling right now is creating your life. Your thoughts and words do not have power at all in your life without your feelings. It is really what you feel that matters.

In any moment you are giving positive thoughts or negative thoughts. You are giving either positive feelings or negative feelings.

All your feelings are a degree of love. You are feeling good because you are full of love, or you are feeling bad because you are empty of love.

If you think, I can't stand my co worker, that is a thought expressing a strong negative feeling you have about your co worker. The consequence would be that your relationship with your co worker will continue to get worse. If you think, I have fabulous people who are my business associates, you are expressing a positive feeling about the people whom you deal with in business. As a consequence, your relationship with your business associates will continue to get better.

It is very important that you become aware of what you are thinking. Your feelings reflect what you are giving. Don't continue to struggle to change the circumstances of your life. Give love through your good feelings and what you desire will appear. You must give good feelings first. You have to be happy to give happiness. When you give and feel happiness, you receive happy things! Whatever you desire to receive in life, you must give first.

Everyone is searching for happiness. If you are not feeling good and you want to change the way you are feeling or if you want to raise your good feelings higher, take a few minutes and go through a mental list of everything you love and adore. You can do this anywhere. It is very simple, and the effect in your life will be amazing.

At the beginning of each month, I urge you to make a written list of everything you love. I am talking about everything you possibly can think of. Include the people you love, places you love, cities you love, colors you love, sports you love, material things you love. You get the picture! Just think of all the things you love to do and list them.

You must be alert to feel the love of everything surrounding you. You have to be aware of everything that is around you to love; otherwise you will miss things. Make a conscious effort to notice as many things around you that you love, as much as you possibly can each day. Your job is to love as much as possible everyday, and turn away from the things you do not love. Your tomorrows will overflow with the untold happiness of everything you want and love.

It is impossible to feel sad or have negative feelings when you are being grateful. Gratitude is the bridge to love. It is the bridge from negative feelings to harnessing the force of love. Gratitude is one of the highest expressions of love. Every time you feel grateful you are giving love.

I'm letting you in on one of the most unknown secrets in the universe. Every time you are giving love through your feelings, words, or actions, you are adding to your magnetic field. The more love you are giving, the greater and more powerful your magnetic field become, which means you become more able to attract the things you love. When you continually live your life by loving, you will get to the point where your field is so positive and strong that you can have a flash of something you imagine, and within no time, it appears in your life. You see how powerful you are! God has given you the ability to think and feel. That is your dominion over all creation.

By harnessing the force of love, you can attract to you whatever you want or change what you do not want, whether it be your health, money, or relationships—anything. Remember, the creation process will always be the same: Imagine it, feel it, and receive it!

Use your imagination to connect you to what you desire. At the same time, feel love for what you desire. Your desire and the feeling of love will create the magnetism. The magnetic power will draw what you desire to you. Desire is a feeling of love; since you must give love to receive love, desire what you want with all your heart.

Now I dare you to push your imagination to the limits, and imagine the best and highest that you possibly can! Just know that whatever desire you can imagine already exists. You can change whatever you desire in your life by harnessing the greatest power in the universe. It is just that simple: Give love!

Remember life is supposed to be fun. When you are having fun, you are feeling great and you receive great things.

FOCUS YOUR MIND ON LOVE

Clarity of mind means clarity of passion, too; this is why a great and clear mind loves ardently and sees distinctly what it loves.

–Blaise Pascal

Here is the secret! Trick your mind by asking questions. No I'm not talking about asking someone else; I'm talking about asking your mind. If you want to truly feel the power? Ask God, universe, spirit! Remember they all are the same, just your preference of reference. This is one way to stay alert.

Ask questions such as: What can I see that I love? How many things can I see that I love? What else is there that I love? Are there more things

I can see that I love? What can I hear that I love? When you ask your mind questions, your mind can not help itself; it gets busy right away to give you the answers. Yes! It stops other thoughts immediately to come up with the answers to your questions.

The secret to continue to walk in this power is you must continue asking your mind questions regularly. The more questions you can ask, the more you will be in control of your mind. You will have your mind working with you and doing what you want it to do, instead of working against you. Your mind only takes off on its own if you are not telling it what to do. Your mind is a powerful and magnificent tool you can use, but you must be in control of it. Instead of letting it distract you with out of control thoughts, you want your mind to help you give love.

Love means to commit oneself without guarantee, to give oneself completely in the hope that our love will produce love in the loved person. Love is an act of faith, and whoever is of little faith is also of little love.

–Erich Fromm (1900-1980)

CONCLUSION

"There is an 'INTELLIGENT MIND' that knows all.
When you understand how to connect YOUR MIND to the
INTELLIGENT MIND, all you desire is yours for the asking!"

–Kanina Johnson

ACKNOWLEDGMENTS

First and foremost, I give all praise to God, my Heavenly Father, for giving me the strength, knowledge, understanding, insights, and wisdom to place my thoughts in written form to help empower other lives.

Thank you, Kevin, my husband, for your continual love toward me. It took me a year to write *Walk in Your Power*. Throughout the year, there were many nights you went to bed without me or awakened in the morning without me physically in the bed because I was writing my present thoughts at the moment.

I thank you, Kevin, for allowing me to be truly me. I always remember that you once told me: The sad thing about you, Kanina, you do not know how smart you are. You know what, baby? I know now!

Thank you, Kayla, my daughter. There were many times I was writing instead of devoting precious time to you.

Thank you, Kevin and Kameron, my sons. There been many times I should have been doing something to help you, but I was writing.

I knew placing my thoughts in written form would empower all of us.

I thank God continually to empower me and my family beyond our wildest dreams.

Thank you, Keishea Pitts, my sister, for believing in me. I know you thought I was crazy at times for the way I think and my behavior. You knew I loved to use my imagination. I bet you don't think I'm crazy now!

Thank you, Jeremy D. Brown, my Publisher for believing in me. You saw the creativity inside of me when others didn't. I truly have great love toward you for all that you have done for me. You have made a dream of mine come true.

Thank you, No Limit Publishing Group, for helping my book come to life. I am sending sincere gratitude and love directly to Jeremy Brown, President/Founder; Chris J. Snook, Editor-In-Chief; Kandi Miller, Vice President of Operations; Jana Uptagraft, my Personal Author Specialist (Hey, Jana! Thanks for helping me keep sanity of my book writing project); Ryan Anderson, Graphic Designer; and Christine Whitmarsh, Managing Editor.

CPSIA information can be obtained at www.ICGtesting.com
Printed in the USA
LVOW032041301111

257284LV00001B/1/P